PROJECTIONS, EXPECTATIONS, SEPARATIONS, JUDGMENTS, & REJECTIONS

The Invalidation of You and the Destruction of Your Relationships

BY GARY M. DOUGLAS

WITH CONTRIBUTIONS FROM DR. DAIN HEER

ACCESS
CONSCIOUSNESS®
PUBLISHING

Projections, Expectations, Separations, Judgments, & Rejections

The Invalidation of You and the Destruction of Your Relationships

Published by:

Access Consciousness Publishing, LLC

www.accessconsciousnesspublishing.com

Contribution from Dr. Dain Heer

Printed in the United States of America

1st Edition

Foreword

Have you ever seen those little rectangular pieces of candy called PEZ Juniors? They pop out of a plastic dispenser in the form of a cartoon character's head. Dr. Dain Heer used a bit of poetic license to invent an acronym for projections, expectations, separations, judgments, and rejections, calling them "PESJRs." PESJRs are as common as those little rectangular candies used to be and they are as destructive to your success in creating your life as those candies could be to your teeth.

This book about projections, expectations, separations, judgments, and rejections is based on a series of teleclasses I facilitated with a group of people from around the world—the United States, Australia, Europe, India, and beyond.

In the course of our conversations, we often used the Access Consciousness Clearing Statement® to destroy and uncreate the projections, expectations, separations, judgments, and rejections that are creating the limitations and contractions in our lives. When you first read the clearing statement, it may twist your head around a bit. That's our intention. It's designed to get your mind out of the picture so you can get to the *energy* of a situation.

Basically, with the clearing statement, we're addressing the energy of the limitations and barriers that keep us from moving forward and expanding into all of the spaces we would like to go. The clearing statement is: Right and Wrong, Good and Bad, POD and POC, All 9, Shorts, Boys, and Beyonds®. There is a brief explanation of what the words mean at the end of the book.

You can choose to use the clearing statement or not; I don't have a point of view about that, but I do want to invite you to try it and see what happens.

There's a whole different world out there if you're willing to be that different world.

If you're not doing the world based on your projections and expectations, you get to see what is in front of you and you get to change anything. But you stop yourself from having it all with your projections and expectations.

Contents

Chapter One

PROJECTIONS AND EXPECTATIONS SEPARATE YOU FROM YOUR AWARENESS

Whenever you are doing projection and expectation of any kind, you are separating, judging, and rejecting anything that would give you awareness. You're eliminating your awareness. That's pretty severe, isn't it?

Gary: Hello, everyone. Welcome to our series of calls on projections, expectations, separations, judgments, and rejections. Let's start by talking about what these things are.

What Are Projections, Expectations, Separations, Judgments, and Rejections?

Projections and expectations are what you think someone else will do even if they aren't going to do it. A *projection* would be "This man is perfect for me." An *expectation* would be "He will have the same point of view about me that I have about him. He'll think I'm perfect for him."

Judgment is any fixed point of view or any conviction that someone or something has to be a certain way. *Separation* occurs once you do a judgment of any kind. You separate yourself from the person or thing you judge—even if it's you. *Rejection* is dismissing or refusing something.

If the other person doesn't have the same point of view you do, they have to separate, judge, and reject you. Or you have to separate, judge, and reject you because the other person is separating, judging, and rejecting you.

Awareness Is the Place Where No Point of View Is Necessary

Whenever you are doing projection and expectation of any kind, you are separating, judging, and rejecting anything that would give you awareness. You're eliminating your awareness. That's pretty severe, isn't it?

Class Participant: Gary, what is awareness?

Gary: Awareness is the place where no point of view is necessary. When you are aware, you have the ability to see and to perceive, to know and to be, and to receive the totality of something in a way in which you don't have to come to conclusion.

Class Participant: I realize I have been trying to get awareness "right." I see that I have had no idea what awareness really is—because awareness can't be right or wrong.

Gary: That's correct. Go back through your life and look at all the places where you knew you shouldn't do something but you did it anyway, and it turned out exactly as you thought it would. That's a time when you were aware and you denied your awareness.

Awareness never comes from believing what people *say;* it always comes from watching what they *do*. Watch what they *do* and you will gain awareness. Watch what they *say* and you will be distracted from what is actually going on. This is where you eliminate your capacity for infinite choice and infinite possibility.

I never have any projections, expectations, separations, judgments, or rejections of anyone. I am always perceiving rather than believing. I am always capable of adjusting according to the moment. I don't believe what people say. I am aware of what's coming out of their head. I am only surprised when they do what they say.

> How many projections and expectations are you using to create the separations, judgments, and rejections of you are you choosing? Everything that is times a godzillion, will you destroy and uncreate it all? Right and Wrong, Good and Bad, POD and POC, All 9, Shorts, Boys, and Beyonds.

Other People's Projections and Expectations of You

Most of us have a lot of things projected at us at an early age, and those projections and expectations can have adverse effects on our body and being. Before the age of two, you do not perceive any difference between you and your parents or the people around you, and you take on their thoughts, feelings, emotions, and points of view. Then when you reach adolescence and seek to rebel against your parents, you are also rebelling against you—because you've made those projections and expectations part of who and what you are.

Someone asked me, "Is it possible to do something to permanently destroy any connection to other people's projections, expectations, separations, judgments, and rejections?"

I said, "Yes, it's called awareness!"

Class Participant: Can you say more about that? I feel like running away from the projections and expectations of other people.

Gary: Well, one of the projections and expectations in this reality is that you have to get married and have 2.5 kids. You're supposed to do things in a certain way, right? But you never could live by that, could you? What would it be like if you were willing to create from what you know instead of whatever everybody else projects and expects you should choose and be?

I don't care if anybody else agrees with me. I don't care if anybody else gets it. I don't care what occurs here. I am going to create something one way or the other.

Interesting Point of View

Class Participant: That's the awareness I'm beginning to step into. It's a huge awareness for me, to not run away from other people's projections of what I'm creating. Their expectations are just an interesting point of view.[1]

---

[1] "Interesting point of view" is an Access Consciousness tool that you can use to neutralize projections, expectations, or judgments by reminding yourself that whatever the projection, expectation, or judgment is, it's just a point of view that you or someone else has at this moment in time. It's not right or wrong or good or bad.

3

Gary: Yes, their projections and expectations are just projections and expectations. They don't mean anything.

> All the projections and expectations you've defined as meaningful are the things that keep you from being everything you are. Everything that is times a godzillion, will you destroy and uncreate it all? Right and Wrong, Good and Bad, POD and POC, All 9, Shorts, Boys, and Beyonds.

What have you suppressed in order to live by the projections and expectations of others?

Class Participant: Wow.

Gary:

> Everything you've suppressed based on the projections and expectations of others, will you destroy and uncreate all those? Right and Wrong, Good and Bad, POD and POC, All 9, Shorts, Boys, and Beyonds.

> How many of the projections and expectations of you that you have defined as meaningful are the things that keep you from being everything you are? Everything that is times a godzillion, will you destroy and uncreate it all? Right and Wrong, Good and Bad, POD and POC, All 9, Shorts, Boys, and Beyonds.

How much have you suppressed you to live by the projections and expectations of others?

> Everything you've suppressed to live by the projections and expectations of others, will you destroy and uncreate all that? Right and Wrong, Good and Bad, POD and POC, All 9, Shorts, Boys, and Beyonds.

Class Participant: I've been doing "Interesting point of view," but it hit me yesterday that I don't think I've really been doing it. To really do it, you have to be pissed off that you have points of view, right?

Any time one of these things comes up, just say: "Interesting point of view." It helps to distance you from it. You don't align and agree with it—and you don't resist and react to it. You just allow it to be what it is, which is no more than an interesting point of view.

Gary: No. I just know that every point of view I have is a limitation, so I don't do points of view. I ask, "Okay, what's next? What else is possible?"

Class Participant: You've said that having a point of view cuts off your awareness. I don't see how a point of view does that. Is it that you don't ask questions when you have point of view because you think you already know what's going on in the world?

Gary: Yes. As soon as you project and expect, you think, "Oh, I know what's going on here." I never project and expect that I know what's going on. I always look at what I have to deal with. Everything is always a question for me. Nobody has it right. People only think they do. I don't think I have it right. If I think I have it right, all I'm doing is setting myself up to lose.

> How many projections and expectations of your rightness are you using to guarantee the losing you will be choosing? Everything that is times a godzillion, will you destroy and uncreate it all? Right and Wrong, Good and Bad, POD and POC, All 9, Shorts, Boys, and Beyonds.

For me, there is no rightness. There is no wrongness. There's just "Interesting point of view" and "What else can I choose?"

Class Participant: Rightness or wrongness is also a point of view.

Gary: Yeah. Rightness is just a point of view. "I'm right, so this is the way it should be done."

> How many projections and expectations are you using to create the crappy life you are choosing? Everything that is times a godzillion, will you destroy and uncreate it all? Right and Wrong, Good and Bad, POD and POC, All 9, Shorts, Boys, and Beyonds.

Class Participant: Thank you, Gary.

Projecting and Expecting Failure

Class Participant: I have a few concerns related to my work and my desire for money. I was practicing as a chartered accountant in India, but it was not going well. I closed down my office and decided to work from home. Then I tried for a job but I didn't get it. Then I moved, and my family resisted it. I'm still not creating the profit I want. What is this? What can I do to change this? Can it be helped?

Gary: You've just talked about how you're a failure. Is that at all real to you?

Class Participant: Yes.

Gary: You're projecting and expecting failure. It could be that someone in your family is projecting and expecting your failure as well. The end result is that you will separate, judge, and reject you. They can also separate, judge, and reject you, and you will align and agree with that point of view and make it even worse.

> All the projections, expectations, separations, judgments, and re- jections you're using to make sure you have no success, will you destroy and uncreate all that? Right and Wrong, Good and Bad, POD and POC, All 9, Shorts, Boys, and Beyonds.

Class Participant: Thank you, Gary.

What's Actually True for Me?

Class Participant: Once when I used to teach, I was invited for dinner to the home of one of my students and I didn't want to go. Was that rejecting them if I really didn't want to go?

Gary: No, it was an awareness that it was not going to turn out well. Did you ask what their purpose was in inviting you?

Class Participant: They were appreciative of me and they wanted to have me over to dinner. But they weren't necessarily a family that I wanted to visit.

Gary: What was their purpose? You didn't ask what their purpose was, did you?

Class Participant: Literally ask them? Or energetically ask?

Gary: You were projecting and expecting that you had to go there because they appreciated you. Was that awareness—or was that con- clusion?

Class Participant: I guess it was conclusion. That's what they told me.

Gary: Yeah. They said, "We appreciate you so much," but you didn't want to go. You didn't question what they really had in mind or why would they do this. Many people say that they want things or they're going to do things or they're going to create things, but is that really what they want? You project and expect that if somebody says something then what they say must be true. That's a projection and expectation that everybody speaks the truth.

But if everybody looks at everything through their own judgments of their own reality, is anybody speaking the truth? No. They're speaking through their projections and expectations, their separations, judgments, and rejections of everything.

> Have you had a projection and expectation that people will tell you the truth, the whole truth, and nothing but the truth, so help you God? Everywhere you bought that crock of shit, will you destroy and uncreate it all? Right and Wrong, Good and Bad, POD and POC, All 9, Shorts, Boys, and Beyonds.

Class Participant: So does that mean that I expected they were not telling the truth?

Gary: If you decide they are telling the truth and they want to honor you by having you over for dinner, and you then don't want to go, what awareness are you refusing?

Class Participant: Oh. Okay. I get it.

Gary: You're believing what they say and you're making that the truth rather than asking, "What's actually true for me here? Do they really want to honor me or are they trying to get something else out of me or...?" And after you went there for dinner, did you feel better, worse, or the same?

Class Participant: I didn't go. I made up an excuse.

Gary: So you wouldn't have to go! That's because you knew they were lying.

Class Participant: But I got caught up in not wanting them to feel I was rejecting them.

Gary: Were you rejecting *them*? Or were you rejecting *your awareness* of what was actually true? And is it a projection and expectation that you have to feel bad if you don't deliver what somebody wants from you?

Class Participant: That.

Gary: Yeah, that!

> How many of you are trying to deliver some projection and expectation somebody has put on you, thinking that way they won't separate, judge, or reject you? Everything that is times a godzillion, will you destroy and uncreate it all? Right and Wrong, Good and Bad, POD and POC, All 9, Shorts, Boys, and Beyonds.

Is anybody beginning to see how this works?

Class Participant: It's so twisted!

Gary: Really? I never noticed!

Class Participant: I keep getting myself trapped. I tend to take things literally.

Gary: How's that working for you?

Class Participant: Well, I didn't go to dinner, but I felt awkward and bad.

Gary: You felt awkward and bad about it! Yep, that's terrible. You're a terrible person.

Class Participant: Thanks, Gary. I get it now.

Gary: You've got to get clear about how this works. How many of you have tried to expect and project somebody to tell you the truth?

> If you try to project and expect somebody to tell you the truth, they get to lie to you. Everything that is times a godzillion, will you destroy and uncreate it all? Right and Wrong, Good and Bad, POD and POC, All 9, Shorts, Boys, and Beyonds.

I never expect anybody to tell me the truth! I'm always in question. I ask: "What's this person actually saying? What's this person actually doing?"

Class Participant: If you expect someone to be decent to you, then you're setting them up to...

Gary: Use you. Isn't that fun? Because when you project and expect anything, you're separating, judging, and rejecting your awareness.

Nobody's Speaking What's True

Class Participant: Never trusting that somebody's going to say something that's true—that has to apply to pretty much everybody on the planet, because we don't even know what's true for ourselves. You facilitate each and every one of us every time we speak and we get clearer on what we actually believe to be true. So nobody is speaking what's true.

Gary: Pretty much, because nobody's willing to look at what's true. They are looking at everything in their life from projections, expectations, separations, judgments, and rejections. What if you didn't look through your projections and expectations, your separations, judgments, and rejections?

Class Participant: I would imagine you'd start seeing what's true for you and you'd be able to ask people questions to get them to see what's true for them.

Gary: No. No. No! It's not about getting people to see what's true for *them*. Your projection and expectation is that you can get people to see what's true for them. I don't do projections or expectations, separations, judgments, and rejections because I'm trying to get somebody to see a point of view nor am I trying to see what their point of view is. I'm only interested in getting the awareness that I want.

You're not acknowledging what you know, because every time you do a projection or expectation about what's going to happen, what's that going to create besides a self-fulfilling prophecy?

Class Participant: I get it. I'm starting to see what is created by every thought and point of view we take.

Gary: You just said the most important thing that's going to be said on this call. We *take on* these points of view. We don't *question* our points of view—ever. If you have no points of view and no projections, expectations, separations, judgments, or rejections, you can be aware of everything and change pretty much anything.

Projections and Expectations That People Throw at Kids

Class Participant: What comes up for me when you talk about projections and expectations are the projections and expectations that people throw at kids who've been labelled with ADD, ADHD, OCD, autism, and that kind of stuff. In the book Would You Teach a Fish to Climb a Tree? *we talk about asking those kids to be true to who they are and at the same time to give their parents or teachers what they require to make their life easier. And to never make somebody else someone they're not. It's like we're saying, "Don't become the projections and expectations people are putting on you. Be you and figure out how to tap into another way of being." Is that right?*

Gary: Yeah, and figure out how to manipulate the people who do that!

Class Participant: Exactly! The kids are way more aware and know way more than the adults or the judgmental people who are throwing that stuff at them.

Gary: Watch. Be aware. You've got to be willing to see the way everything works.

Class Participant: This makes it so clear! Thank you.

Living Up to Expectations (or Not)

Class Participant: My brother and his wife have four kids. The two oldest are girls and when they were growing up, one of them was labelled and identified as the beauty. The other one was identified as the smart one. The girls overruled their awareness and became what they were labelled. Both of them are stunningly beautiful and brilliant, yet they wouldn't allow themselves to have the qualities projected on the other one, because it didn't fit into the projections and expectations that were thrown at them. The oldest one became an alcoholic and the youngest one dresses like a bag lady. Does this mean that you never really see people when you project and expect?

Gary: Yes. As long as you're doing projections and expectations of anyone, you can never see what's actually true.

Class Participant: It seems that when people project their expectations onto me, I make sure to disappoint them so they don't control me. There's something twisted about that.

Gary: Why would you want to make other people's dreams come true?

Class Participant: Well, I don't, obviously, because when they compliment me, I go the opposite direction. It's as if I'm saying, "No! Don't put those projections and expectations on me!"

Gary: You have the projection and expectation that you've got to make other people's dreams come true.

Class Participant: That's not working out too well! How do I stop that?

Gary:

> You cannot fulfill other people's dreams or desires. Everything that is times a godzillion, will you destroy and uncreate it all? Right and Wrong, Good and Bad, POD and POC, All 9, Shorts, Boys, and Beyonds.

Class Participant: If someone asks me to do something and they're expecting me to perform at a high level, even though I could perform at that high level, I somehow screw it up so I don't have to live up to their expectations.

Gary: I'm impressed. Are you impressed?

Class Participant: I don't know if my intentions are really helping me.

Gary: Who cares? You keep trying to pretend that you care about what other people think.

Class Participant: I do.

Gary: Do you truly care?

Class Participant: Not really.

Gary: So stop pretending. You're projecting and expecting that you *must care,* which means you *don't actually care.*

Everything you're doing to project and expect your caring, will you destroy and uncreate it all? Right and Wrong, Good and Bad, POD and POC, All 9, Shorts, Boys, and Beyonds.

"I Would Never Do That!"

Class Participant: I find myself expecting things of other people. Sometimes when I see people doing stuff, I say things like, "I would never do that!"

Gary: The moment you do projection and expectation, you cut off your awareness.

Class Participant: How do I stop doing that even though I know I'm doing it and I shouldn't be doing it?

Gary: Say: "Everything that makes me think this is real, destroy and uncreate it all." Projections and expectations are *never* reality! They are just projections and expectations. Nothing more.

Class Participant: Do you know what I mean when I say we have habitual behaviors and we keep doing them even though we know better?

Gary: Yes. Habitual behaviors are where we put projections and expectations on automatic repeat.

All the projections and expectations you have on automatic repeat, will you destroy and uncreate all those? Right and Wrong, Good and Bad, POD and POC, All 9, Shorts, Boys, and Beyonds.

You do projections and expectations over and over again as though the projections and expectations will create a different result.

Family

Class Participant: People around me, even my family members, are always projecting something onto me. I'm aware that I pick up stuff from them.

Gary: You have to look at it and ask: "Is this a projection and expectation?" You're from India, right? Are there any projections and expectations about your being an Indian man?

Class Participant: Yes, lots.

Gary: All of those projections and expectations—and luckily there are no projections or expectations about Indian women, or Chinese women, or American women, or Aussie women, or women in general, or projections and expectations about men! Oh yeah, there are!

> All of the projections you have about any of that, any of the gender identification, will you destroy and uncreate them all? Right and Wrong, Good and Bad, POD and POC, All 9, Shorts, Boys, and Beyonds.

Class Participant: When I'm around my family, I feel like they have an image of me that has nothing to do with me. I feel like it's totally irrelevant to me.

Gary: Why are you projecting and expecting them to be family? You have some projections and expectations about what family is.

Class Participant: It is weird. They have an idea about me that has nothing to do with me. I want to be free of that. I don't know what it is and I don't know what to do with it.

Gary: What are you trying to create as real for you that actually isn't? Do you have a nice family who loves you?

Class Participant: I think it's conditional. That's not very nice.

Gary: Conditional love is not actually love. So, I'm going to ask again, do you have a loving family?

Class Participant: Umm.

Gary: Yes or no?

Class Participant: They can't be both?

Gary: No.

Class Participant: Okay, then I have to say no.

Gary: But you keep expecting them and projecting them to love you because they're family.

Class Participant: Aha, I see that.

Gary: What do they do for you? Do they take care of you and love you? Or do they reject you and judge you?

Class Participant: They reject me and judge me.

Gary: You're trying to look for how your judgment of them creates separation, judgment, and rejection. You're not seeing that you've already decided that they reject you. So rather than being aware of what's actually possible, you keep looking for how they're not going to do that. How about doing something different?

What if you started looking at who they really are? Your projection and expectation is that one day they will love you because they're family. Is that looking at what family is? Or is that not acknowledging what family is?

> How many projections and expectations of family are you using to receive the separation, judgment, and rejection of you they are choosing? Everything that is times a godzillion, will you destroy and uncreate it all? Right and Wrong, Good and Bad, POD and POC, All 9, Shorts, Boys, and Beyonds.

Ah, how nice.

> How many projections and expectations of family are you using to receive the separation, judgment, and rejection of you they are choosing? Thank God you're the only one who has this! No, you're not! Everything that is times a godzillion, will you destroy and uncreate it all? Right and Wrong, Good and Bad, POD and POC, All 9, Shorts, Boys, and Beyonds.

You put your projections and expectations out there and your family ends up liking you better, right?

Class Participant: Um, I don't think so.

Gary: Correct, they don't. You project and expect that you love them. You keep expecting that if you are kinder and better to them, they will stop separating, judging, and rejecting you. Has that ever turned out to be true?

Class Participant: No.

Gary: This is where you've got to give up looking to the past, or to your experience, or to your projections and expectations. You're expecting something to show up that doesn't ever turn out to be true. Guess what? In order to create the pretense that it's all going to turn out right, you've got to cut off your awareness. Is that how you want to live your life?

Class Participant: No, I don't want to live like that.

Gary: So who are you really judging, rejecting, and separating from?

Class Participant: Me.

Gary: Yes. Is that a good idea? Is your family going to like you better if you separate, judge, and reject you?

Class Participant: No, they aren't.

Gary: What would happen if you were willing to be as great as you actually are?

Class Participant: I probably wouldn't care what anyone thought, especially my family.

Gary: That's great.

"Other People Are Like Me"

Class Participant: So if we're in relationship with someone, whether it's family or someone else, are we seeing them based on our projections and expectations?

Gary: You think that other people are like you. If I project and expect that other people will be like me, am I delusional or am I completely and utterly crazy? Or am I all of those things?

Everywhere you've done projections and expectations that others are like you, will you destroy and uncreate all that? Right and Wrong, Good and Bad, POD and POC, All 9, Shorts, Boys, and Beyonds.

This is one of the hardest things you're ever going to get: Nobody is like you. You are unique unto yourself.

When we do a projection and expectation about the way other people are like us, it keeps us from seeing the separations, the judgments, and the rejections others are doing of us. And we then must do the separation, judgment, and rejection of us—because they are not like us.

> Everything that brought up times a godzillion, will you destroy and uncreate it all? Right and Wrong, Good and Bad, POD and POC, All 9, Shorts, Boys, and Beyonds.

Are you beginning to see that projections and expectations may be a much bigger deal than you thought they were? They're huge, because they have so many ramifications. We keep trying to see how we fit into something. But if you are trying to see how you fit, are you actually being aware? Or are you projecting and expecting how you fit?

> How many projections and expectations are you using to create how you fit, which keep you from fitting in this reality? Everything that is times a godzillion, will you destroy and uncreate it all? Right and Wrong, Good and Bad, POD and POC, All 9, Shorts, Boys, and Beyonds.

> What have you made so vital about projections, expectations, separations, judgments, and rejections that keep you separating, judging, and rejecting awareness? Everything that is times a godzillion, will you destroy and uncreate it all? Right and Wrong, Good and Bad, POD and POC, All 9, Shorts, Boys, and Beyonds.

Do you see that when you do projection and expectation, you have to function in separation, judgment, and rejection? You have no other choice.

Class Participant: For me, there's some connection between thinking everyone is the same and everyone is like me...

Gary: How many projections and expectations are you using to make other people like you?

Class Participant: "Like me" in terms of liking me as a person or "like me" as in similar to me?

Gary: You're trying to define what "like" equals. If somebody is like you, will you like them? If you like somebody, do you assume they're like you?

Class Participant: Oh. Yes.

Gary:

> Everything that is times a godzillion, will you destroy and uncreate it all? Right and Wrong, Good and Bad, POD and POC, All 9, Shorts, Boys, and Beyonds.

You're not willing to look at what's actually true for people. You say, "Oh, I like this person. Cool." What does that mean? It means nothing. I like lots of people. I like my ex-wife. Do I want to live with her? No! I like my children. Do I want them to live with me? No! I like my horses. Do I want them sleeping with me? No! Everything has its place.

You guys say, "I like this person," and then you forgive them all their trespasses. You fall in love with somebody and you assume they're going to think like you because you fell in love with them. Is that person ever really going to think like you?

Class Participant: Clearly not.

Gary:

> How many projections and expectations do you use to believe in people thinking like you are you choosing? Everything that is times a godzillion, will you destroy and uncreate it all? Right and Wrong, Good and Bad, POD and POC, All 9, Shorts, Boys, and Beyonds.

Be in Question

Class Participant: So how can we be with people?

Gary: You have to be in question. You have to ask: "What's really going on here? What's going on for them?" Be in question. You keep trying to come to the conclusion "Oh, they love me because..." They love you because of what? Your projections and expectations about family are not related to an ounce of truth! How are you ever going to see what's true?

Class Participant: Do we choose our families based on projections and expectations?

Gary: Yes, isn't that great? "They must have loved me in some life-time!" or "I will teach them how to love!" Have you ever seen a little kid who tries to do funny things to make his family look at him, love him, and be happy with him?

Class Participant: Yeah.

Gary: Does it work? No, they find the kid annoying. His projection and expectation is "I can teach them how to love." How many of you are projecting and expecting you can teach someone—your wife, your husband, your significant other, your dog, or your cat how to love?

Everything that is times a godzillion, will you destroy and uncreate it all? Right and Wrong, Good and Bad, POD and POC, All 9, Shorts, Boys, and Beyonds.

Class Participant: I have a good family, but my mother can't accept Access. I listen to telecalls in Australia a lot of the time, and she doesn't accept that.

Gary: She obviously cares for you, right?

Class Participant: Yes.

Gary: She does? Is she helping you achieve your dreams or is she trying keep you in line with where she wants you to be?

Class Participant: Yes.

Gary:

All the projections and expectations creating that as your reality, will you destroy and uncreate it all? Right and Wrong, Good and Bad, POD and POC, All 9, Shorts, Boys, and Beyonds.

Do any of you get that you're using the projections and expectations of others to determine what your life and your reality are supposed to be?

Everything that is, let's destroy and uncreate it all. Right and Wrong, Good and Bad, POD and POC, All 9, Shorts, Boys, and Beyonds.

Gary: Okay, everyone, we're going to call it quits here today. Please start looking at everything you're doing and ask: "How many projections and expectations am I using to create projections and expectations so I can separate, judge, and reject myself?" because that's what you do. You reject being when you do projection and expectation.

Class Participant: Wow!

Class Participants: Thank you, Gary.

———

If you have no points of view and no projections, expectations, separations, judgments, or rejections, you can be aware of everything and change pretty much anything.

Chapter Two

GIVING UP BEING RIGHT

*The purpose of projections and expectations is not to be
aware but to be right. You'd rather be right than free.
I'm not kidding here. You've got to see this.
You can be right or you can be free. Which do you choose?*

Awareness Goes Beyond Being Smart

Gary: Hello, everybody. Let's start with a question.

Class Participant: Yesterday I came to the awareness that I make myself wrong in order to make other people right, so that when their rightness doesn't work for me, I can call them stupid and make myself smart.

Gary: Are you projecting and expecting you to be *smart* rather than *aware*? When you project that you must be smart, you eliminate awareness.

Class Participant: Yeah, I realized I am the stupid one, trying to make myself smart. When I was a little girl, the projection was that kids were stupid. When you're a kid, you know nothing. So I made it my goal to be smart. I got straight A's and the whole bit.

Gary: Even with the straight A's, were you considered smart?

Class Participant: No, never smart enough.

Gary: No, you were still a kid. Awareness goes beyond being smart.

Whenever you project and expect that you are smart, or you will be smart, or you need to be smart, are you looking at what is possible? No, because you are doing everything through separations, judgments, and rejections.

Class Participant: And I have to do what everybody else thinks is smart, which is not the smart thing.

Gary: Which is not about whether or not you're smart. It's about doing what everybody else thinks.

Class Participant: Yes. Yes! Oh my goodness! I'm not the only one who does this, am I?

Gary: Yes! You're the only one.

Class Participant: (Laughing) It's crazy!

Gary: Yes, it is crazy. That's why I am doing these calls. I watch people doing this stuff and I say, "That's frigging crazy! Why would you choose that?"

People say, "Oh, this is the way it's done." Say what? This is the way it's done? What does that have to do with anything? It has to do with nothing!

Class Participant: Do I just do the process of clearing projections and expectations on being smart and being stupid?

Gary: Yeah. First of all, if you're smart, you cannot be aware. The projection and expectation is that "smart" equals "greater than awareness."

Everywhere you've gone to "I must be smart in order to be greater than awareness," will you destroy and uncreate all that? Right and Wrong, Good and Bad, POD and POC, All 9, Shorts, Boys, and Beyonds.

Class Participant: That's awesome. Thank you.

Gary:

What have you made so vital about projections, expectations, separations, judgments, and rejections that keeps you separating, judging, and rejecting awareness? Everything that is times a godzillion, will you destroy and uncreate it all? Right and Wrong, Good and Bad, POD and POC, All 9, Shorts, Boys, and Beyonds.

Victorious over Wrongness

Class Participant: Sometimes when I do lots of clearings, and particularly in the last couple of days leading up to this call, I feel like everything is opening up. Everything is vast and free, and at the same time, there's an awareness of massive grief, mourning, and loss as I see lie after lie that I and others have been creating. I ask, "What the hell is real? What is actually real?"

Gary: Would you like me to answer that? Nothing is real.

Class Participant: (Laughs) Right. That's what I came to. Nothing is real. Trying to describe these things is like trying to fit the sky into your handbag. But there's a loneliness and a temptation to make a story about it being wrong…

Gary: It's always wrong to be aware.

Class Participant: Right. It feels wrong, doesn't it, because you're not going along with anybody's stories—yours or anyone else's.

Gary: You're not going along with anything. You're just creating! It's always wrong to create. What part of that don't you get?

Class Participant: (Laughs) Right!

Gary: There's another thing that goes along with this: If you have no projections, expectations, separations, judgments, and rejections, you can actually be happy!

Class Participant: Right! And how wrong would that be?

Gary: It's always wrong to be happy. Unhappiness makes you right. Happiness makes you wrong.

Class Participant: I've been so right my whole life. Now I'm so wrong!

Gary: You're projecting and expecting that you must be wrong in order to be right. Happiness is the greatest travesty on planet Earth!

Everything that is times a godzillion, will you destroy and uncre-ate it all? Right and Wrong, Good and Bad, POD and POC, All 9, Shorts, Boys, and Beyonds.

Class Participant: Is this the beginning of the next cycle of trying to make myself wrong so I can make myself right again so I'm victorious over the wrongness?

Gary: Victorious over the wrongness. I love that!

Class Participant: It's "This is not going to pull me down. I'm going to beat this!" It's a perpetual cycle of proving I'm right and then being wrong. I go to the wrongness so I can prove I'm right again.

Gary: Oh, lordy! It's a never-ending story, in order to create rightness. It's your life as you currently live it.

What have you made so vital about projection, expectation, sepa-ration, judgment, and rejection that keeps you eternally seeking the never-ending story of the wrongness that makes you right? Everything that is times a godzillion, will you destroy and uncreate all that? Right and Wrong, Good and Bad, POD and POC, All 9, Shorts, Boys, and Beyonds.

Rightness Becomes Your Drug

Class Participant: That's the conundrum, isn't it? The belief that there is a right or a wrong is the crux of this whole thing. I'm playing in a place where I'm wrong for what reason? Wrongness becomes my drug and then rightness becomes my drug. I'm just swapping one drug for another, which is really the same drug with a different name.

Gary: Rightness is the drug!

Class Participant: But you have to go to wrong in order to get to right. What is that "hit" you get off rightness? What is that?

Gary: You'd rather be right than free. Freedom is being able to choose anything. Rightness means you have chosen.

Class Participant: Oh! Yes!

Gary: And it's way more fun to be right than to be free—except it actu-ally isn't.

Class Participant: And it only works for a few minutes.

Gary: I know. Isn't that all you need? A few minutes of rightness?

Class Participant: Just another hit.

Gary: Thirty seconds of rightness is worth everything in life. You would kill people for that thirty seconds.

Class Participant: I have! I have eaten people for breakfast! I can picture myself with a toothpick, picking them out of my teeth.

Gary: I ate a bushel of rightness.

Class Participant: (Laughs) Why is that so fun?

Gary: Because you're an idiot?

Class Participant: Yeah!

Gary: You'd rather be right than free. I'm not kidding here. You've got to see this. You can be right or you can be free. Which do you choose?

Class Participant: Somewhere in the mind, a switch has gone off that says being right is being free because you feel a high from it.

Gary: It makes you better than everybody else.

Class Participant: Yeah, wow. I can see where that habit was formed. It's easy to see because I was always being told about the wrongness of me and I fought back against it with "I'm not wrong. I'm not bad." I was fighting for what I felt was my freedom.

Gary: If you're wrong, you're bad. But if you're right, are you good? Or are you not bad?

Class Participant: You're just not bad.

Gary:
> Everything that is times a godzillion, will you destroy and uncreate it all? Right and Wrong, Good and Bad, POD and POC, All 9, Shorts, Boys, and Beyonds.

The Table Scraps of Not Being Wrong

Class Participant: You end up fighting to get back on par. You're not even getting ahead. It's just that your head is no longer under water. It's not living. I get it totally. When you're right, you're just not wrong. So there you are, feeling awesome to have the table scraps of not being wrong at the end of the day.

Gary: Not starving to death.

Class Participant: Right. Not starving to death. I love that. Thank you. That's beautiful.

Gary: I'm not starving to death. I'm just not full. I'm not as stupid as I think I am. I'm just as stupid as I know I am. How's that working for you all?

Class Participant: Not anymore! I'm lit up and feeling really big as we're having this exchange.

Gary: You have to get that the choice is to be right or to be free. Most of you would give up freedom for rightness every frigging time! Good idea? Bad idea? Bad idea! Don't be right. The only freedom there is in life is the ability to choose. Which one are you most willing to have? The ability to choose? Or the rightness of your point of view?

Class Participant: In the United States, at least, how often do we hear about people dying for freedom or dying for their country and making that so right and so valuable?

Gary: You'd give up your life to make your *country* free but you won't give up your rightness to make *you* free. Why is it that your freedom is not as important as your rightness? What if you were more willing to be free than you were willing to be right?

Have You Ever Been Accused of Being an Asshole?

Class Participant: That is a huge thing, because when you think you're right, you're a total asshole to everyone around you. You think you're doing something that is right and that everyone should see how right and great you are, but everyone just sees what an asshole you are, that you think you're right. I guess that's not a question. It's a statement.

Gary: That was a statement. That was an acknowledgement of what is. Have you ever been accused of being an asshole?

Class Participant: Yeah, and I think I couldn't see it at the time because I thought everyone was like me.

Gary: You projected and expected that everyone was like you, so when you're being an asshole, you expect people to see how you're not really an asshole, because you're not really an asshole—you're just right. And why don't people see how right you are and just follow you the way they should?

> Everything that is times a godzillion, will you destroy and uncreate it all? Right and Wrong, Good and Bad, POD and POC, All 9, Shorts, Boys, and Beyonds.

Dain and I were recently in Italy and we looked at a castle that we were thinking about buying. It was going to take a lot of restoration and repair. Before I made an offer on it, I wanted to know what it was going to take to restore it. The lady who showed us the castle said, "I speak perfect English." She didn't. She just thought she did. Her projection and expectation was that she could handle all of this stuff.

My reality was "I need to know what's actually true here, and I don't trust anybody to tell me the truth, the whole truth, and nothing but the truth!" I don't believe anybody knows the things they think they know. They just think they know and they want my money. It's not a *projection* and *expectation* that they want my money; it's an *awareness* they want my money. Do they really want to give me the information I want? Or do they want to give me the information that will allow them to get the money they want from me?

Class Participant: The second.

Gary: The second one, yes. I hired one of our translators in Europe, and I said, "I want this information translated to me and I want to talk to this guy and that guy. If that does not occur, I'm not buying this place. This is not acceptable to me. It goes my way, or I'm on the highway. Goodbye." Why was I doing that? Because I'm an asshole? Or because I was aware that the woman who showed us the castle was more interested in being right than she was in being aware.

All the projections and expectations that others put on you about how they're right that you keep trying to buy or see as true or real, will you destroy and uncreate all that? Right and Wrong, Good and Bad, POD and POC, All 9, Shorts, Boys, and Beyonds.

The Desire to Control Everything

Class Participant: It seems like my life is driven by the desire to control everything. It's the unwillingness to just surrender and let go.

Gary: Yeah, control everything and get everything right!

Everything you've done, every projection and expectation you have that makes you right and keeps you in control, would you consider destroying five percent of them—but no more? Everything that is times a godzillion, will you destroy and uncreate it all? Right and Wrong, Good and Bad, POD and POC, All 9, Shorts, Boys, and Beyonds.

How many projections and expectations are you currently holding onto, to make sure your life does not grow beyond your ability to control it? Everything that is times a godzillion, will you destroy and uncreate it all? Right and Wrong, Good and Bad, POD and POC, All 9, Shorts, Boys, and Beyonds.

Class Participant: I have an image of Garfield, the cat, hanging on the wall with his claws dug in. It's that paralysis thing. It's stupid. It's insane!

Gary: Yes. You do projections and expectations because you're trying to make sure that nothing has to change and everything will remain the same, so you get to have all the control and be totally right.

If You're Willing to Be Totally Free, Losing Is Not a Reality

Class Participant: You talk about being willing to lose everything. How does what you're saying here relate to that?

Gary: If you're willing to be totally free, losing is not a reality. Most of you are not willing to be free enough to have the choice to lose or the choice to win. You have to ask: "What do I want? The freedom to choose? Or the rightness of my point of view?"

You've got to look at this on your own and ask: "What is most valuable to me? The rightness of my point of view? Or the freedom to choose?" This is the place you have to look from and choose from. If you had the freedom to choose anything, what would you choose? Most of you would choose to be right over choosing to create.

Class Participant: Not anymore!

Gary: Good. Now we're getting somewhere! Look at it and ask: "What am I choosing here?" and "I would choose this for what reason?"

The Only Thing That Is Real and True Is What We Make Real and True

Class Participant: Gary, there's a moment where the projections and expectations seem so real. I've lived every single day of my life as if they're totally real. Is understanding or knowing that they're not real the first step in unhinging from all of this?

Gary: You have to realize that everything is the opposite of what it appears to be and nothing is the opposite of what it appears to be. This is an important tool. Once you get that everything is the opposite of what it appears to be and nothing is the opposite of what it appears to be, choice becomes possible.

Class Participant: I hear you say that, but I don't really know what it means.

Gary: It means "Everything is the opposite of what it appears to be and nothing is the opposite of what it appears to be." It means the same thing.

Class Participant: Oh. Everything we think is real isn't?

Gary: Everything you think is real isn't, and everything you think isn't real isn't either.

Class Participant: So what is?

Gary: Nothing.

Class Participant: Like you said earlier, nothing is real.

Gary: Nothing is real. When I was told, "Everything you've ever thought was real or true is a lie or an implant[2]," I said, "What?! If everything I think is true or real is a lie or an implant, then how many lies and implants am I living from?"

When you begin to see that, you can create your business a different way, you can create possibilities a different way, you can look at anything you desire and ask: "Okay, how do I get what I really desire?" and "Which of these do I truly desire?"

Class Participant: When I hear this stuff, an amazing energy hits me. What is that? Are you guys channelling stuff or is this the process of the awareness, the awakening?

Gary: When I first started doing Access, a lot of the stuff was channelled. Then as I began to work with people, things would come out of their mouths and I would say, "Oh my gosh, that's true!" The phrase "Everything is the opposite of what it appears to be and nothing is the opposite of what it appears to be" came out of the mouth of someone I was working on. I said, "That's so true!" I saw that we create stuff as real and true when it isn't, and we create things as not real and true when they are. So is anything real and true? No. The only thing that is real and true is what we make real and true.

Class Participant: That's the key thing. It's what we make it, which is another way of talking about the projections, expectations, judgments...

Gary: It's a way of acknowledging projections and expectations, because none of them are real. We've decided they're real. That's all it is. We decide something is real; therefore, it becomes real. Does that make it real? No.

---

[2] An implant is something that is energetically entrenched or established in your universe. It is designed to be triggered by the events of your life and to create distractions that keep you from being all that you can truly be and having the life you would truly like to have. Implants are the reason we believe we have no choice in anything. For more information about implants, read *Living Beyond Distraction* or listen to the Distractor Implants telecall series.

What energy, space, and consciousness can you be to create a reality beyond this reality with total ease? Everything that is times a godzillion, will you destroy and uncreate all that? Right and Wrong, Good and Bad, POD and POC, All 9, Shorts, Boys, and Beyonds.

What's the Purpose of a Problem?

What would it be like if you didn't ever think there was a problem? What if there are no problems except the things we *make* problems. Why do we make things problems? When we make something a problem, we do it so we can live in this reality, as though this reality is all we desire.

Class Participant: Do we make problems so we get to believe in this reality, so we make it more real?

Gary: What's the purpose of a problem?

Class Participant: To solve it.

Gary: Yes, to have something to overcome. You have a problem so you have a reason for living, so you can justify everything you choose. What if there was no justification for choice? What if there was just choice? You put projections and expectations out there to justify why you choose something, and in so doing, you don't have true choice. You only have choice based on justification.

Everything that is times a godzillion, will you destroy and uncreate it all? Right and Wrong, Good and Bad, POD and POC, All 9, Shorts, Boys, and Beyonds.

What if you chose because you could?

Justifying the Rightness of Your Point of View

Class Participant: Are we trying to justify the rightness of our point of view? Is that what you're saying?

Gary: Everything you do is based on justifying the rightness of your point of view. "I hate him because blank, blank, blank." Okay? "I love him because blank, blank, blank." Say what? What if you loved him because you could? What if you chose because you could? What if what you truly desired was because you truly desired it?

We try to justify our reason for everything. People spend money and they go to reason and justification for why they chose to spend the money. I don't do that. I say, "Okay, I spent the money."

People ask, "Well, why did you spend it?"

I say, "Because I did."

People ask, "Yeah, but what are you going to get out of that?"

I say, "I already got."

They ask, "What do you mean 'You already got?'"

I say, "I spent it because I did."

They say, "Yeah, but you have to have a reason for spending that kind of money."

I say, "No, I don't. I just spent it."

They say, "Well that's crazy!"

I say, "Yes. By your standards, but not by mine."

You project and expect that you have to justify what you choose. You don't ever get to choose because you choose.

> Everything that is times a godzillion, will you destroy and uncreate all that? Right and Wrong, Good and Bad, POD and POC, All 9, Shorts, Boys, and Beyonds.

Heaven and Hell

Class Participant: What happens when people have projections and expectations about what's going to happen when they die? If they think they will go to heaven or to hell, what happens when they die?

Gary: Whatever they've chosen beforehand.

Class Participant: So their expectations become real?

Gary: Yes, of course!

Class Participant: That's shit.

Gary: Your projection and expectation is, "I've got to be real. I must be real. I've got to prove to everybody else I'm real." You want to be real, don't you? You justify every choice you can make, by the fact that you're real, based on the judgment you have of you. You do judgment and separation and rejection in order to prove that you're real.

Class Participant: That was a big one.

Gary: Yes, I know.

"I Must Be Right, I Must Be True, I Must Exist"

Class Participant: Do we also do projection and expectation based on our judgments?

Gary: Well, of course. How else can you be right? Without your judgments, are you right or wrong?

Class Participant: You're…

Gary: Notice you can't answer the question.

Class Participant: If you have no judgments, you're neither right nor wrong.

Gary: That's correct. If you have no judgment, there is no right or wrong, there's just a choice.

Class Participant: So you actually project and expect from a space of…

Gary: Of judgment and making yourself right. Why is making yourself right the most important thing there is?

Class Participant: Because in this reality, if you're not right, you don't exist.

Gary: If you're not right, you don't exist! If you've decided you're not right, you don't exist; therefore, you have to prove you're right in order to exist. That's a projection and an expectation of existing. It's not an awareness of what might be possible.

Class Participant: How much of what we're doing and being in our life is about having to prove something?

Gary: All of it!

Class Participant: (Laughs) Oh my God!

Another Class Participant: That we're real. That we're right.

Gary: We're real and we're right; therefore, we exist. "Where's my choice?" Oh, yeah, I gave that up for rightness. "Where's my life?" Oh, I gave that up for existence! "Where's everything I desire?" I gave that up for rightness, existence, and…what else? If you motivate yourself with being right, that gives you lots of choice, doesn't it?

Class Participant: No. It gives you this one-shot, one-choice reality.

Gary: Yeah. It's the one-choice reality. My choice is "I must be right." My choice is "I must be true." My choice is "I must exist." None of it has anything to do with choice. It has everything to do with projections and expectations. And then there are separations, judgments, and rejections to prove it's true.

> Everything that is times a godzillion, will you destroy and uncreate all that? Right and Wrong, Good and Bad, POD and POC, All 9, Shorts, Boys, and Beyonds.

Dain: If loving you guys is wrong, I don't want to be right.

Class Participant: (Laughs) Thanks, Dain!

Class Participant: I just got that I'm trying to be right by doing everything I can to avoid judgment.

Gary: Yeah, isn't that great?

Class Participant: No.

Gary: No! If you're trying to avoid judgment, all you're doing is making yourself not wrong.

Class Participant: Right. It's just justification. And it's causing so much chaos!

Gary: Aren't you proud? "I can make myself so right that I screw up my whole life! Wow. Am I powerful!"

Class Participant: Thank you so much. This is what I was trying to see.

Gary: You've got to be proud that you can screw yourself up this well!

Class Participant: (Laughs) Oh my God!

Gary: If you screw yourself up this well, can you imagine what would happen if you used this same energy for you?

Class Participant: Exactly.

Gary: Do I have a different point of view or what?

Class Participant: (Laughs) We are so grateful for that.

When Is It a Projection? And When Is It an Awareness?

Class Participant: If, as you said, awareness doesn't have a right or a wrong, how do I know whether something is an awareness?

Gary: Because it's not right or wrong.

Class Participant: So when is it a projection? And when is it an awareness?

Gary: Awareness always creates choice. Right or wrong justifies everything you choose, and everything you do, and everything you are. Basically it boils down to this: Awareness creates a place where you have choice. Right or wrong creates a place where you justify everything you choose. If you never had to justify your choice, what choices would you have?

Class Participant: All choice.

Gary: Yeah. So, when you decided that you loved your husband, did you have to justify it? No, you didn't. You just knew. Then it became a choice, right?

Class Participant: I had a sensation in my body that didn't have anything to do with thinking. Is that what knowing is?

Gary: Yep, because you know what you want to choose! And you continued choosing, right?

Class Participant: Correct.

Gary: Do you have to justify your choices?

Class Participant: No, I don't think about it.

Gary: Yeah. You don't have to think about it. When you have to justify, you have to think about it. And if you're thinking, you're not doing awareness. If you're justifying, you're not doing awareness.

Class Participant: The other day a person we were doing business with asked for a refund due to a family emergency. When I read the information in the request, I said, "This person is lying to me." I knew. I didn't have a question or a doubt about that, yet everyone else did.

Gary: Yes, because you have more willingness to be aware than you're willing to acknowledge.

Class Participant: Well, now I am wondering, "Well, was that true? Was that a lie?"

Gary: It doesn't matter whether it's real or true. For me, it's never about what's true or real. It's about how I want to handle it. I ask: "What's going to make it easiest on me?"

"I have a family emergency" is a justification. Why is the person justifying? She wants her money back. A guy once came to a class of mine, and he said, "I don't think I believe in this."

I said, "You don't have to believe in it. Why don't you try it and see what works? If it doesn't work, I'll give you your money back the next day."

He did the class and afterwards he said, "Wow, this works!"

I said, "Cool."

Four weeks later, he said, "I want my money back."

I said, "Wait a minute. I told you that you could have your money back the next day if it didn't work, and you didn't say it didn't work."

He said, "Yeah, but it's not working now."

I said, "The reality is that you want your money back because you need the money."

He said, "Well, yeah. So you should give me my money back."

I said, "No, I'm not going to. That was not the agreement."

He said, "Well, I will make your life miserable."

I said, "Feel free. Do you think you're going to make me feel miserable over money? No. It's a different reality for me."

Do You Want Total Choice?

Class Participant: I've noticed that when I do or say things, there's usually an expectation involved. Even when I ask a question, there's an expectation embedded in it.

Gary: Do you ask a question based on the projection and expectation of the answer that you want?

Class Participant: I'm coming to the awareness that I do that a lot. Yes. So, how do I recognize that I'm doing that?

Gary: If you're doing a projection, expectation, separation, judgment, or rejection, you've eliminated all choice except those. You are trying to be right. You have to give up being right! Do you want total freedom? Stop trying to be right! Do you want total choice? Stop trying to be right! Do you want total possibility? Stop trying to be right!

If you're trying to do rightness, you have no choice; you can only do rightness. You've already made your choice: "My choice is to be right. Therefore, even if it's not working, I'm right."

> What are you trying to make right about this stupid-ass point of view that keeps you from having everything you desire? Everything that is times a godzillion, will you destroy and uncreate all that? Right and Wrong, Good and Bad, POD and POC, All 9, Shorts, Boys, and Beyonds.

Dain: Gary, you created this teleclass series in the first place because you recognized that projections, expectations, separations, judgment, and rejections are a major element of what's destroying our capacity to be present, create, and choose. They're a major element of what puts us into judgment of everything and everyone we're connected to, and they stop us from being everything we know we can be. And that's not a judgment! That is total awareness.

Choose. Choose. Choose.

Class Participant: Can we make projections and expectations playful in some way? I don't want to judge myself or make myself wrong for having them. Is there a way I can play with them?

Gary: Here's a way you can play with them: I want you to project and expect that you're going to make a million dollars tomorrow.

Class Participant: Okay, I like that.

Gary: Now make it happen!

Class Participant: Well, f--k! (Laughs)

Gary: Oh f--k. Yeah. Projections and expectations are not playful. They're the "Oh f--k!" of your life.

Class Participant: So if I have them in everything I do and they're constant, what do I do?

Gary: Get the fact that they're not working and say, "F--k this shit. I'm not going to choose this anymore." Or, continue to screw up your life—whichever you like best.

Class Participant: Yeah, I haven't decided that yet.

Gary: Yes, I know. You like your projections and expectations because they keep you from creating.

Class Participant: And choosing.

Gary: They keep you from choosing, from creating, from having the life you'd like to have—but they make you right. That's why you want

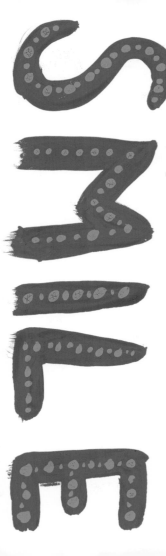

to play with them—because they make you right! "My projections and expectations are right. That's why I want to play with them!"

Class Participant: (Laughs) Totally!

Gary: How do I f--k me over? Let's count the ways!

Class Participant: Are you saying, "Just choose by doing it? Give up having to be right"?

Gary: Choose, choose, choose. "If I don't have to be right, what choices do I have?"

Class Participant: You know that point where you have a negative expectation? You say, "I'm going to do the uncomfortable thing. I'm expecting something negative and I'm going to do it because I have to be right." Are you saying to just give that up and choose not to be right?

Gary: No, don't do that. Make yourself right. It's more fun.

Class Participant: (Laughs) Thanks Gary. I got it. Wow. That's cool.

Gary: You think you have to be right, you have to be perfect, you have to be correct, you have to be all kinds of things, but you're not willing to recognize "That's a frigging stupid choice!" because if you acknowledged that it's a stupid choice, you'd have to make a different one. And you don't want to make a *different* choice, you want to make the *right* choice!

Class Participant: Gary, you always makes this sound so easy. Could I ask Dain a question? Dain, how did you get to the point where you released projections and expectations?

Dain: I started realizing they were destroying my life and everything I could create, and one day I said, "Enough! No more!"

At first I would notice after the fact that I'd just done an expectation or a projection, and I'd say, "Shit!" It's so familiar when you do it. I'm not a person who has spent my life judging. The only thing I would ever judge was me. But I did a lot of projections and expectations because I thought that's how you created things. I thought that if I projected and expected it, then it would show up.

After having conversations with Gary about this, I realized how destructive projections and expectations are, and I made the demand to not do that anymore. Every time one would show up, I'd POC and POD[3] it. And when it would show up again, I would POC and POD it again. After a while of doing that, I started to recognize the energy when it would show up, and I wouldn't go into it anymore. That was a lot easier, and I would only have to POD and POC some of the time. It got me to the place where I had a different choice.

Class Participant: Thank you.

Gary: What Dain wanted was more choice. You have to get to the place where you're more interested in choice than being right.

Class Participant: Great. Thank you, both, so much.

Gary: You're welcome. That's the end of our call for today, folks. Thanks, everyone.

Class Participant: Thank you, Gary!

———

The only freedom there is in life is the ability to choose.
Which one are you most willing to have?
The ability to choose? Or the rightness of your point of view?

---

[3] "POD and POC is shorthand for the clearing statement.

Chapter Three

Judgment Does Not Create: It Destroys

How many projections and expectations are you using to make real the judgments you are choosing to believe?

Gary: Hello, everyone. Let's start with a question.

Are You Judging and Rejecting You?

Class Participant: One of the members of the business group I run is a man who likes to wear makeup and dress very differently. There are some challenges between him and a second guy in the group. And because I'm the one who's taking the lead in the group, the second guy thinks that I should do something to make the first guy change. He's also judging and separating from me, and I notice that I'm doing that with him.

Gary: When people are doing projections and expectations of you, you will usually judge and reject you, thinking that's the way to avoid the judgment and rejection they're doing of you. You judge and reject you in order to not be judged and rejected—so who's judging and who's rejecting? Oh, you are. It goes both ways.

Class Participant: What would you do in this situation?

Gary: I would say to each person in the room, "Okay, obviously there's some judgment going on here. What's your judgment of this person? And this person? And this person?" As you do that, it will become very obvious to everyone that guy number two is doing judgment as a way of creating separation from everybody else. Most people use separation, judgment, and rejection as a way of not getting connected or close to people—and they are always the people who blame everybody else for not being close to them.

Class Participant: Thank you.

"You're Right. I'm Wrong. How Can We Change This?"

Class Participant: There's a particular person I'm avoiding. I'd rather put my finger in a blender than have a conversation with this guy. Talking with him feels like it creates nothing except judgment of me and my situation.

Gary: Hold on, hold on, hold on. How right would you have to make this guy in order to get him to stop making you wrong? You're projecting and expecting that you're going to be made wrong and judged. Yes or no?

Class Participant: Totally.

Gary: How right do you have to make somebody in order for them not to make you wrong? The only thing he's doing by making you wrong is avoiding being wrong himself. You need to recognize that most people are idiots who want only one thing—to be right! Ninety-nine percent of the population desires only one result in life. To be right! So tell him, "I'm sorry. You're right. I'm wrong." Ask: "How can we change this?" not "How can I tell you how wrong you are?" not "How can you tell me how wrong I am?"

"You're right. I'm wrong. How can we change this?" Just keep saying that until he says, "No, you're not wrong. You're just mistaken." Once he says that, you are in control. I have tried for years to teach you how to be in control. You keep trying to avoid being in control by doing confrontation. You have judged that confronting somebody is going to change something. Does that actually work?

Class Participant: No.

Gary:

> How many projections and expectations of the result you want in life are you using to avoid getting the change that would give you everything you desire? Everything that is times a godzillion, will you destroy and uncreate it all? Right and Wrong, Good and Bad, POD and POC, All 9, Shorts, Boys, and Beyonds.

You think your job is to get a *result.* No. Your job is to get a *change.* That's all you want. You want change—not a result.

Class Participant: So should I pick up the phone and have a conversation with this guy that goes nowhere?

Gary: No! You can make it go somewhere by *not* making him wrong and *not* making you wrong, but by simply telling him that you are wrong. He's an idiot who has to be right all the time. That's why he judges you.

> How many projections and expectations of the results you want in life are you using to avoid getting the change that would give you everything you desire in life with total ease? Everything that is times a godzillion, will you destroy and uncreate it all? Right and Wrong, Good and Bad, POD and POC, All 9, Shorts, Boys, and Beyonds.

As long as you are projecting and expecting that this person is going to judge you and be upset with you, guess what's going to get created?

Class Participant: That.

Gary: Yes, that! If you have the point of view "How can I change this?" Do you have to change all of it? Do you have to change him? No. Do you have to change you? Maybe. Do you have to change the situation? Yeah. How can you change the situation without him recognizing what an asshole he is? By acknowledging that this man is an asshole and he will never change. When people are assholes, I say, "Okay, they're assholes." I don't care. Am I going to change me to fit their reality? No. But you will—because you will avoid calling him.

"I So Get What You're Talking About"

Class Participant: What would conscious leadership look like in a conversation with him?

Gary: Say "I so get what you're talking about" because that makes him, from his point of view, see how right he is. From your point of view, you see he's an idiot. Let me ask you a question: When somebody farts in your presence do you say, "Oh my God, you farted?" No. Do you say, "Oh my! What was that?" No. You pretend it didn't happen.

What comes out of this guy's mouth? Farts. He's a mouth farter. It's called judgments.

> How many projections and expectations are you using to make real the judgments you are choosing to believe? Everything that is times a godzillion, will you destroy and uncreate it all? Right and Wrong, Good and Bad, POD and POC, All 9, Shorts, Boys, and Beyonds.

Class Participant: Thank you for that. I've always wondered why people believe judgments are real. I just realized that it's not that they believe the judgments are real. It's that they project and expect the judgments must be real.

Gary:

> How many projections and expectations are you using to make real the judgments you are choosing to believe that are not real? Everything that is times a godzillion, will you destroy and uncreate it all? Right and Wrong, Good and Bad, POD and POC, All 9, Shorts, Boys, and Beyonds.

If you project and expect that someone is going to judge you and you avoid them, all you're doing is getting away from what you've decided you don't want to deal with—and that's a projection and expectation that there is something you need to avoid.

Class Participant: When I'm in a conversation with this person, he asks questions in a way that makes me feel like I'm being dissected. It's like he's pushing me in a particular direction.

Gary: You're still trying to defend the point of view that he's trying to get you.

Class Participant: Yes, there is a feeling that he's trying to get me. It creates nothing other than a mess in the conversation.

Gary: Yes. You've projected and expected that it's going to turn into a mess. So guess what it's going to turn into! How many projections and expectations do you have that this man is greater, smarter, brighter, and more real and true than you?

"Wow, That's Very Interesting"

Class Participant: Ah. Probably a couple. So should I just do "Interesting point of view" whenever this comes up in a conversation?

Gary: Yeah. All you have to do is say: "Wow, that's very interesting." Instead of answering his questions, say: "That's interesting. I never thought of it that way," or "I don't actually know what my point of view about that is. Can you talk to me in a day or two so I can think about it?" I don't answer questions. Why do you?

Class Participant: I'll try that on.

Gary: All you have to do is play with it. You have so many projections and expectations about this guy that all you're going to do is create disaster—because you've decided he's stronger, brighter, more brilliant, and greater than you. How many projections and expectations do you have to make others greater than you? The only one who is greater than you is *me*!

(Laughter)

I led you into that one! You've got to become aware. This guy is trying to lead you into a trap.

Class Participant: Yes! Exactly.

Gary: But, how can you be trapped if you're not willing to be trapped?

Class Participant: Right.

Gary: I'm never willing to be trapped, so I'm always willing to say whatever someone needs me to say in order for them to feel good about themselves.

45

Class Participant: Thank you.

"Really? I Don't Remember That."

Class Participant: What happens if someone tries to hold you to something you said? What do you do with that?

Gary: You say, "Really? I don't remember that. I must be getting to be more of a blonde or more of an airhead," or "I must have more gray hairs than I realize." Never let somebody trap you. No one gets to do that unless you give it to them, and in order to do that, you have to have the projection and expectation that they are somehow greater, brighter, and more dynamic than you are.

> All the projections and expectations you use to create others as greater than you and everything that is times a godzillion, will you destroy and uncreate it all? Right and Wrong, Good and Bad, POD and POC, All 9, Shorts, Boys, and Beyonds.

Receiving an Accusation

Class Participant: Could you talk about receiving accusation with ease?

Gary: Why would you want to receive it with ease?

Class Participant: I thought we had to be willing to receive all energies.

Gary: Yes, we do. And I'm asking you, why would you want to receive an accusation when it's so much easier to reject it?

Class Participant: Is that what I'm doing?

Gary: Yes.

Class Participant: Could you explain how to not do what I'm doing?

Gary: What's more important to you? To realize you're wrong? To realize you're right? Or to make yourself absolutely, brilliantly wrong when you're right, and right when you're wrong?

Class Participant: The last one.

Gary: Apparently you're the only one who has this unconsciousness. It's nice to know that you're the only one who's screwed up and everybody else is perfect!

Class Participant: Yeah. I'm having the awareness that if I see all the projections and expectations of others into my universe, then I'm being or doing something that I'm not. I'm asking for more ease with that.

Gary: No, you can't have ease with that. You have to be screwed up!

Class Participant: I'm demanding ease with it.

Gary: I'm sorry. You can't have more ease in life.

Class Participant: I'm demanding it, Gary! What else is possible?

Gary: Who gave you permission to demand that your life be ease, joy, and glory?

Class Participant: (Laughing)

Gary: Did any of you notice that as I started trying to goad her into a different point of view, she was saying, "What? What are you doing?" She wasn't saying, '"Oh, f--k you, Gary! I will too." Now, why would I want her to get to the point where she says, "F--k you, I will too!"?

Because the war with yourself is over at that moment. The nice thing about fighting yourself is that you always know that you can win! What? What do I mean you can always win? You can always win the war against yourself because you will always lose. Why would you always lose? Are you positive that you're a winner? Are you positive that you're a loser? Or are you positive that somehow it's never going to come out the way you want it to?

Class Participant: I get that I'm more the loser.

Gary: You think you're a loser because you've already decided that you're wrong. Wrongness is always losing, isn't it?

Class Participant: Absolutely, that's my computation.

Gary: The only one good enough to actually lose with is you!

Class Participant: I'm over this now. Could you assist me, please?

Gary:

> What do you love about being a pathetic pile of shit loser? Everything that is times a godzillion, will you destroy and uncreate it all? Right and Wrong, Good and Bad, POD and POC, All 9, Shorts, Boys, and Beyonds.

"I Don't F--king Care How Much You Dislike Me. I Like Me!"

Gary: What do you love about being a pathetic pile of shit loser? If you're a pathetic, pile of shit loser, do you deserve anything?

Class Participant: No.

Gary: Do you deserve all the bad stuff that happens to you?

Class Participant: Yes.

Gary: Do you deserve to see how much other people dislike you?

Class Participant: Yes.

Gary: I'm going to give you a tool: "I don't f--king care how much you dislike me. I like me!"

Class Participant: That's a good tool.

Gary: But you've got to use it.

> Everything that brought up, will you destroy and uncreate it all? Right and Wrong, Good and Bad, POD and POC, All 9, Shorts, Boys, and Beyonds.

If you have the point of view, "I don't care if you like me. I like me," and you don't look for somebody to validate you, you choose what works for you that validates you!

Class Participant: Is that how the Earth is constantly in a state of magic?

Gary: Yes. Because it never judges itself. It says, "I'm beautiful, even if you're f--king me over!" If you get in a relationship and someone f--ks you over, you say, "It's so terrible this person would f--k me over. How could they do this to me? I know they love me."

Or you could get into a relationship and say, "They f--ked themselves over. Okay, fine. Bye."

> Everything that brought up, will you destroy and uncreate it all? Right and Wrong, Good and Bad, POD and POC, All 9, Shorts, Boys, and Beyonds.

Class Participant: All of that protection and all of that fear, and all of that "Who has more? Who has less? Who gave what? Who didn't give what?" All this falls away when you don't have judgments of you.

Gary: All this falls away when you don't have any projections or expectations about anybody having the point of view that they can do something to you or that they shouldn't do something to you. If you have no projections or expectations about anything or anyone, you're always happy with whatever they do.

One of my grandchildren is autistic. Her parents don't want to know that. Autistic kids don't like to look you in the eye and they don't like to touch. Her parents are always telling her, "Give Grandpa a kiss. Thank Grandpa for this. Do this for Grandpa." I say, "Don't do that to her," because I'm willing to look at what is. They're not. They think I'm not going to love her as much if she doesn't do those things. I'm willing to see where she sits and ask, "Why would you make her do this? Why would you make her prove that she loves me by doing something she doesn't want to do?"

I also have that point of view about people I'm in relationship with. Why would I make somebody do something they don't want to do in order to prove something to me? "If you love me, you won't go out and have sex with someone else." My point of view is that if you love me and you find out I'm the best sex you've ever had, you won't have to go off with someone else! And if I'm not willing to be the best sex you've ever had, then you deserve to go off with somebody who's better than I am.

Class Participant: Exactly!

An Asshole Is Just an Asshole

Class Participant: You have talked about how you are willing to be an asshole because you do what works for you. When I see you do that, there's a sense that you're creating something greater. You're not being an asshole just to be an asshole.

Gary: How many projections and expectations do you have about what being an asshole is?

Class Participant: A ton.

Gary: An asshole is just somebody who can fart on command. It's not somebody who's mean and vicious; it's somebody who can shit on your parade if you're willing to let them. Basically, an asshole is someone who farts and walks away! You have all kinds of projections and expectations about what an asshole is.

How many projections and expectations do you have about what being an asshole is that keep you from having the freedom to be the asshole you need to be? Everything that is times a godzillion, will you destroy and uncreate it all? Right and Wrong, Good and Bad, POD and POC, All 9, Shorts, Boys, and Beyonds.

What is your definition of an asshole?

Class Participant: It's someone who's mean, rude, and selfish.

Gary: That's not an asshole. Mean, rude, and selfish are what mean, rude, and selfish are. Being rude is being rude. Being a jerk is being a jerk. Being mean is being mean. If you call those things being an asshole, you're going to be controlled by people willing to do those things—because you're not going to be willing to see that they're mean, rude, and nasty.

Class Participant: That's where I've been getting trapped.

Gary: Yeah. You've got to look at *what is,* not what *you want it to be.* That's the projection and expectation of what you think an asshole is, or what you want an asshole to be, so you can conglomerate that all into one little box of confinement that it is not.

Class Participant: It's wrapped up into this whole courtesy thing about not wanting to offend someone.

Gary: Really? You really don't want to offend people?

Class Participant: No. I don't want to offend people.

Gary: That's because you think being offensive is being an asshole—but that's not it. Being offensive is just being offensive. In order to be everything you are, you have to be willing to be everything you can be. If you define rude and mean and nasty as being an asshole, then you can't be an asshole unless you think you're being mean, rude, and nasty—and you don't desire to be mean, rude, and nasty to everybody, just people who you enjoy being like that with.

Class Participant: It's getting to the enjoying part that I'd like.

Gary: You're not going to have that as long as you're misidentifying and misapplying somebody who's mean, rude, and nasty as an asshole. An asshole is an asshole. People who are mean, rude, and nasty are not assholes. They are just mean, rude, and nasty.

Being Nice—Image or Persona?

Class Participant: You know the "nice" thing? People anticipate that I will be nice and I project the image of being nice. But sometimes I don't feel like being nice...

Gary: Hold, hold, hold. Have you projected the *image* of being nice or the *persona* of being nice? The *persona* is being you. The *image* is trying to be something you're not. Image is "I'm really nice. I'm a good person. I wouldn't do anything mean to you. I would never be mean to you! I would never be bad. I would just be a kind, great person."

If you do the "I'll be a fine, great person" image, people who are mean and vicious will come after you in order to prove the lie you're telling is not true. They will judge you. And that works really well, doesn't it?

So maybe you could just be who you are. If you go back to the guy who has been judging you and say, "Wow, that's an amazing level of judgment you have of me. I didn't realize I was that bad. Thank you so much for caring." Does he care? No. But if you claim that he was caring, then he has to care for you. Put him in a place where he has to do what you want him to do.

Class Participant: The persona.

Gary:

> How many projections and expectations are you using to create the persona of who, what, where, when, why, and how you can be that you aren't, are you using? Everything that is times a godzillion, will you destroy and uncreate it all? Right and Wrong, Good and Bad, POD and POC, All 9, Shorts, Boys, and Beyonds.

If you're doing a persona and you're trying to make that happen, you're actually invalidating you in order to be the image you think people will buy, instead of being you, who everybody will love.

Class Participant: Oooh. I love your classes.

Gary:

> How many projections and expectations are you using to create the persona of who, what, where, when, why, and how you can be that is not real? Everything that is times a godzillion, will you destroy and uncreate it all? Right and Wrong, Good and Bad, POD and POC, All 9, Shorts, Boys, and Beyonds.

Whenever you do a projection and expectation of who, what, where, when, how, and why you are, the image of what you're trying to create with who, what, where, when, why, and how you are limits what you can be. You don't have any other choice than to separate, judge, and reject yourself every time you don't fit that image. And that just locks you up. I'd rather you didn't put yourself in jail without having a jail around you.

Okay, everybody, that's it for today!

Class Participants: Thank you, Gary.

———

How many projections and expectations do you have to make others greater than you?

Chapter Four

MONEY, BUSINESS, AND SUCCESS

*I wish I could say that you can create success by projection
and expectation, but you can't. All you can do with projection
and expectation is create failure.*

Gary: Hello, everyone. I'd like to read a question that has come in.

Differentiating Projections and Expectations from Awareness

Question: I have a question about differentiating projections and expectations from awareness. A business deal I recently negotiated fell through on the last yard line. Ironically, the same day it fell through, another larger deal came through. It would have been difficult if both deals had come in at the same time.

Part of me was relieved the first deal fell through, although I was also disappointed. That was the deal I was most excited about, because it was in Bordeaux. I was projecting that it was going to be totally awesome and open a thousand doors, and I was expecting it to go through. And now I wonder if my projection and expectation before the ink was dry caused it to fall through.

Gary: If you're not willing to see where you're projecting and expecting a point of view and where you're willing to have awareness of a point of view, the two of them are going to come into conflict.

Awareness comes from the willingness to know what you truly desire. It doesn't come through projections and expectations.

"What Exactly Do I Desire?"

My grandson is here and he's yelling at Chris, "Come on, let's play." He thinks everybody should want to play with him. And when he asks, "Will you play with me?" it's hard to say no. From his point of view, this isn't a projection or an expectation. It is a need and a demand. It's exactly what he desires.

You're not willing to look at "What exactly do I desire?" and you've got to be willing to do that. You have to be in the question: "What is this going to create?" As long as you're asking, "What is this going to create?" more creation will occur. And as soon as you start doing projection and expectation about what the result is going to be—the moment you go to result—you start killing the thing.

Anytime you do a projection or expectation, all you can ever create is separation, judgment, and rejection from awareness, from possibility, from choice, from money, from greatness, from that which is fantastic and phenomenal, and from being everything you are.

If you do projections or expectations, you end up rejecting you—because you, as an infinite being, know greater than projection and expectation.

A guy who was doing Access said to me, "I'm so excited. I've got a class going on and ten people coming!"

I said, "That's great. Congratulations."

Well, he went to the class and one person showed up.

He asked me, "What did I do?"

I asked, "What did you project and expect as a result of that class?"

He said, "Well, I knew it was going to pay all my bills, it was going to bring me up-to-date financially, it was going to do this, it was going to do that." The projection and expectation was about those things. It was not about the creation of possibility.

Never count your chickens until you have the cash in your hands. That's how you created the place where the first deal fell through. You had no projections and expectations about the second deal other than it could be a good job. That was an awareness, not a projection and expectation. "This could be a good job and it could take care of a lot of stuff" is different from "I want to have this result. I want to have that result."

You've also got to ask: "What choice do I have that I haven't acknowledged?" Look at the creation. If you look at what you project and expect as a *result,* you've actually completed it; it cannot come to fruition.

The Willingness to Be Successful

Gary: If you're in the question, you have no projections and expectations. You ask: "How is this going to work out?" Let's use my antique business in Australia as an example. I asked, "How the hell do I make this work?" I looked around and I found Chris. I asked him, "Chris, will you consider the possibility of working for the Antique Guild?"

He said, "I'm not sure. Why?"

I said, "Because I think you might like it and I could really use you."

He said, "Okay, fine."

Did I expect him to be successful? No, but I was willing to know that he had the elements of what could create success in his own life. Someone who is willing to create success in their own life is willing to contribute to you and create success in your life too. If you project and expect that they're going to be a contribution, if you project and expect that they're going to be perfect, if you project and expect that they're going to be great, they cannot be that.

Class Participant: So when you see people who can create success in their own life, does that mean they are...

Gary: It means they are willing to be successful. Chris was willing to be successful. The only thing he needed was a format that would allow him to use all the parts and pieces of him that make him uniquely him, with no projection or expectation or trying to get him to do a certain thing. He's one of the best research people I've met in my entire life!

55

If he doesn't know what something is, he'll find out. He's not willing to sit and wait. He doesn't project or expect somebody else to do it. He's willing to do whatever it takes to be the successful person he can be. Few people are.

Class Participant: Do you find that the people who don't get the job done are trying to make you happy rather than create what's possible?

Gary: Yes. They're projecting and expecting what's going to make me happy rather than doing what's going to make them happy. I never ask anybody to make *me* happy. I ask them to make *them* happy.

Class Participant: What are the elements of Chris's willingness to be successful?

Gary: He doesn't desire to be less than himself, ever. He desires to be more at all times.

Chris: I thought it was ambition.

Gary: You're misidentifying and misapplying that ambition is a wrongness. In this reality, you're a bad person if you're ambitious.

Ambition is the need to overcome the limitations that others cannot. Creation is the ability to outstretch anyone and go beyond what anybody else is capable of. You've got to have the ambition to create your life. For most of you, the only real ambition is not to show yourselves as better than others. That's what people consider ambition. But seeing you as better than others is what? Projecting and expecting that you have to be better than others, rather than asking, "What do I really want to create here?"

Class Participant: Could you speak about using controversy to your advantage in order to create?

Gary: Controversy is being willing to never buy anybody else's point of view as greater than yours, but also never confronting anybody or making anybody else defensive so they have to prove the rightness of their points of view.

Class Participant: Nice. I appreciate that.

The Projection and Expectation That Something Will Be Successful

Class Participant: I recently started my own company for the second time. I first started it seven years ago and had some challenges. Recently I was able to get an investor and start it again. I'm not clear on what projections and expectations I have of the company.

Gary: You've got the projection and expectation that the company is going to make money, which has nothing to do with what's actually possible.

Class Participant: Thank you. That's what I was about to say. I'm sure I have expectations that I want it to make money. I failed to do that in the past. I want to reach customers. So how do I not screw that up?

Gary: The way not to screw it up is to ask: "What projections and expectations do I have here and is this really going to work?" Projections and expectations never work.

Class Participant: Okay, I see. One follows the other.

Gary: Yes. You do a projection and expectation and everything follows the projection and expectation. What does that have to do with what is actually true for you?

Class Participant: To be aware, I need to get the projections and expectations out of the way. I think I have started doing that because I want the company to be successful.

Gary: Whenever you do projections and expectations of any kind, you're creating failure—not success. I wish I could say that you can create success by projection and expectation, but you can't. All you can do with projection and expectation is create failure.

What projections and expectations are you using to guarantee the failure of your company are you choosing? Everything that is times a godzillion, will you destroy and uncreate it all? Right and Wrong, Good and Bad, POD and POC, All 9, Shorts, Boys, and Beyonds.

You guys keep trying to come to conclusions about what you need in order to choose the success you are certain your company deserves. Let's see, would deserving be a projection, an expectation, a judgment, or a conclusion? Or all four?

Destroy and Uncreate Everything Your Business Was Yesterday

You've got to destroy and uncreate everything your business was yesterday and then go to the question: "What do I need to create now?" I do that on a daily basis.

Class Participant: How do you destroy and uncreate what your business was yesterday? Just by saying, "I destroy and uncreate everything it was yesterday"?

Gary: Yeah, "Everything this business was yesterday, I now destroy and uncreate it all." It's way too easy, which is why none of you do it!

Another Class Participant: I do it.

Class Participant: I'll do it too!

Gary: Once you start doing it, all kinds of new things will show up and you'll ask, "What am I doing here?" All things become possible when you're willing to have the awareness of all things that are possible.

Class Participant: This area with the company and the money is still very important to me.

The Expectation That You Need to Make Money

Gary: That's an expectation. That's not a question. The basic point of view is "If I desire it hard enough and long enough, it will come to fruition." You haven't had that point of view about any girlfriends you've had, have you?

Class Participant: Yeah, it always comes up! I've learned to not want that as much. But making money is important to me.

Gary: You have the expectation you need to make money.

Class Participant: Yes.

Gary: How many of you have the projection and expectation that you *need* to make money? Not that you would *like* to make money, not that you *can* make money, not that you're *going to do everything you can* to make money, but "I *need* to have money, therefore, blah, blah, blah."

Everything that is times a godzillion, will you destroy and uncreate it all? Right and Wrong, Good and Bad, POD and POC, All 9, Shorts, Boys, and Beyonds.

Class Participant: I have a question about the reverse of that. I don't expect that I need money because I already have money. But then I want more money, and the money doesn't come. What is that? It feels very twisted and bent in my universe.

Gary: You've got a projection and expectation that money will come because you like it.

Class Participant: Right.

Gary: I don't have the projection and expectation that money will come because I like it. I make a demand. I ask: "What's it going to take to create all this money, because I like it and I'm going to have it!" You haven't made a demand on yourself that you will have it—no matter what it takes.

Class Participant: Well, I'm making that demand right now!

Gary:

Everything that doesn't allow that to show up times a godzillion, will you destroy and uncreate it all? Right and Wrong, Good and Bad, POD and POC, All 9, Shorts, Boys, and Beyonds.

Our Past and Our Experience Are Not Equal to Awareness

Class Participant: Gary, do we create projection and expectation from the past?

Gary: Yes, and if you're looking to the past, everything has to be a projection and an expectation—because today is not the past. Today is the future, and you finally got here.

We look to the past as though the past and our experience are equal to awareness—but they are not. So you must do separation, judgment, and rejection of presence, awareness, and question in order to have that experience or the past.

I was once involved in a court case, and my attorneys did a mock trial and surveys to see what people would think of the case and the way it was presented. The people in the survey group had no information about me personally other than a paragraph from an article and a comment by an attorney. Based on that miniscule amount of information, they concluded that I was a controlling son-of-a-bitch who made too much money. Where was that coming from? Their projection and expectation was that if I was living in Santa Barbara, then obviously I had too much money, because only rich people live in Santa Barbara. Is that actually true? I wish it were so, but it's not. Those were projections and expectations. The people had projections and expectations, then they separated from me, judged me, and rejected me. Why did they do that? Because their judgments were more real to them than their awareness.

Only one person out of twenty in the group could actually hear what was being said and question what she was being told. She was the only one willing to use her awareness. The rest of them went straight into the projections and expectations of everything they heard based on their already-existing points of view. They related what they heard to their own life and experience.

Everybody had their projections and expectations. The lawyers had their projections and expectations, the panel who were supposed to be judging the case had their projections and expectations, all of them based on what they call their experience. But the moment you go to *experience,* you come out of *awareness.* Experience is a projection and expectation that you use to determine the rightness of your point of view. It has nothing to do with being aware of what's in front of you.

Rejecting and Separating from Money

The people in the survey group projected that I was too rich and I was a terrible person and a shyster because I was making too much money. I thought it was quite amusing, because through their filter, anybody who makes more money than they do has to be doing it in an illegal or under-handed way. That's how people reject and separate themselves from money.

How many projections and separations are you using to create the separations, judgments, and rejections from money you are choosing? Everything that is times a godzillion, will you destroy and uncreate it all? Right and Wrong, Good and Bad, POD and POC, All 9, Shorts, Boys, and Beyonds.

I get the impression that maybe one or two of you are actually beginning to realize that you're separating, judging, and rejecting money by the projections and expectations about what you have to be, or do, in order to have it. That's not going to create for you, is it?

Holding onto Money

Class Participant: Gary, I have a situation with a client. She paid in full for a six-month package and I gave her a deep discount. The deal was that she could have a refund if she didn't get what she was wanted after the first session. Well, after the first session, she decided she didn't want to proceed and asked for a refund. Something is sticking me here. I would like to get to a place of more space with this.

Gary: Give the money back.

Class Participant: Just give it back?

Gary: You had the projection and expectation that in doing a deep discount you would make money. The only way you're going to make money is if you give somebody back their money and say, "Here you are, no problem. Glad to give back the money. Don't ever contact me again in any lifetime."

Class Participant: I've been sitting with that. I know it's fair and you would probably say that, yet I feel unwilling to do it. I am resisting it. I am trying to get to what is locking that up. When you said to give it back just now, my response was "Okay. I can do that." Why couldn't I just do that myself?

Gary: Because you expected and projected that you would get the money. You decided that you would get the money. And after you decided that you were going to get the money, guess what? You didn't want to give it up. Once you had it, you didn't want to get rid of it. The point of view that you didn't want to get rid of it was locking you up.

When you made the deal with the woman, instead of asking, "What kinds of projections and expectations will this woman have of me?" you asked, "How much money can I get?" Oops.

Class Participant: That's correct. I didn't come from awareness with this one. Thank you for that. I am giving it back as soon as I hang up from this phone call!

Gary: You can write out the check right now while you're on the phone call. I'm going to read a question that has come in.

Question: Together with my four siblings, I own some land and the house where we grew up. It used to be a farm. Now it's a cultivated field rented out to other farmers. It's close to wild nature and has natural resources, yet it is so far north that it is not worth very much in dollars and cents. It is, though, the land I have. We use it for common holidays, but my boyfriend and I hardly ever go there because of the insane people we have to deal with. One of my sisters moved back in without asking any of us if we found that okay. And one of my brothers, the biggest jerk on the planet, is planning to move back there when he retires. He has separated out the best part of the property where he will build his house. If I give this away now then sell my share later on, I will reduce the value of my share of the property. This doesn't feel light to me, and I don't want to give him anything.

On the other hand, there will be hell to pay if I do not sign, and I will probably never go back to visit the house, the land, or the family. I do care about most of them even if I don't like them very much. I am the only one who is thinking about selling my share. I know all the others expect to have it almost for free. What is my best choice here?

Gary: Give them whatever the hell they want and walk away! Who cares? It's a useless piece of land that's costing you money! Give them everything and do it from the point of view "I'm being so generous to you all because I know how much you deserve it." Then go and create some frigging money for yourself. It's bizarre that you want to hold on to this. Look at what's true.

When You Turn Money Loose, More Money Comes

Class Participant: Hey Gary, I gave my client her refund while we were on the phone.

Gary: Great. Doesn't it feel better?

Class Participant: I feel so much better! Thank you. It was so silly!

Gary: I know. We run into this all the time. People are always trying to hold on to money when they get it, as though that's the way to create it. But holding on to it is a projection and expectation that if you turn it loose, you're never going to have any. When you turn money loose, more money comes.

"I Don't Want to Be a Millionaire. I Want to Be Right!"

Class Participant: Once I've got money and I've decided that it's mine and I've decided where it's going, if somebody wants it back for some reason, or they have a family emergency, or my mum wants it, I auto-matically go to "No! You're not getting my money." That's a big one for me. What can I do about that? It's hard for me to give them the frigging money. Should I start doing a practice once a month and give them at least a little bit of the money they're asking of me? Will that help me?

Gary: No. Ask them how many times they will kiss your ass in order to get it.

Class Participant: (Laughs) Will that help alleviate the pressure I feel about holding on to it?

Gary: Maybe. You could ask: "How many times would this person be willing to kiss my ass to get me to release my money to them?"

Class Participant: Does this have anything to do with projection and expectation of money or rightness? I hold on and decide it's mine and they're not getting it…

Another Class Participant: It sounds like it would be so much fun to get those people to kiss your ass.

Class Participant: Does it?

Gary: Okay, would it be fun to get someone to kiss your ass?

Class Participant: (Laughs) Yes.

Gary: It's fun to torture people with the idea you will give them money if they kiss your ass well enough.

Class Participant: Is this situation different from the person who didn't want to give her client the refund?

Gary: You're talking about people who are trying to get your money.

Class Participant: Well, some of them have given me money and I've decided that it's mine after they've given it to me. And then they've used a lame excuse—or lies—to try and get it back from me and I refuse. So it is a similar situation, although I'm never going to see these people again. It happens with family too, when my brother or my mum wants money. They haven't given money to me. They just want to take it from me. So, my situation is similar to hers, except she's trying to build a business with people and I couldn't care less about the people who have given me their money.

Gary: What's going to be easier? To give them money and move on with your life? Or to continue to hold on to the money as though that money is the most valuable thing to you?

Class Participant: It's totally what you're saying and what that other person just did. That's why I'm asking you: What is a good way for me to start alleviating this so I can just get the hell out of there and move on to getting that money back twofold, or threefold, or a hundredfold?

Gary: Give them the money. Or say, "Unfortunately I'm strapped at the moment. I'll pay you $50 a month for the next 500 years."

Class Participant: (Laughs) The idea of messing with these people and asking them to kiss my ass lightens it up. I don't think just giving it back to them is going to work for me, though, as hard-headed as I am.

Gary: You have to decide that you really want to do it. You keep trying to come to a projection and expectation about what makes you right. You're only interested in being right. You're not interested in being free.

Class Participant: I've seen that. I have built defense systems around being right. They're starting to unhinge during these last two calls—except for this one particular thing about money, where I keep holding on. It keeps me from being a millionaire. You know?

Gary: Yeah. Isn't it great? "I don't want to be a millionaire. I just want to be right!" You've got to stop trying to be right. You've got to start being what works. So what works? Does "I'm right" work? No. I'm a pragmatist. If it's going to work, I'll do it. If it's not going to work, I ain't going to do it.

Class Participant: You have to come out of judgment to be able to do that, don't you?

Gary: That's correct, which means you have to get rid of all your projections and expectations, because they are just judgments. They're the ways you make yourself right. Are you interested in being right? Or are you interested in being free?

Class Participant: Thanks, Gary.

"I Know I Can Make Money but…"

Class Participant: I had a plan that I was going to write some books and it was going to take roughly four years. People are saying that it would be a drain on my money, it would create a lack of security for my spouse, and it would be something he couldn't take. For me, it was something that I was naturally going to do, and it wasn't going to be a problem.

Gary: Yes I know. For you, it wouldn't be a problem. You know you can make money. Yes or no?

Class Participant: Yes.

Gary: Do other people know they can make money?

Class Participant: Oh. No. So they project and expect that I can't… because they can't.

Gary: Yeah. If they can't do it, how are you going to do it? You'll turn a corner and make a dollar because you can, because you like money.

Class Participant: Is that where I pick up the projections and expectations and start feeling doubt in myself?

Gary: Yes. Most people don't know that they can recover from any-thing. This is one of the things I've talked about for years. I've been totally broke four times. I've started from nothing four times. But I don't stay broke.

Class Participant: *It's not your reality.*

Gary: It's not my reality. Broke doesn't work for me, sorry. I like money. I want more, thank you very much.

Class Participant: *Thanks, Gary. I do know that I can make money.*

Be Interested—Not Interesting

Class Participant: *(speaking rapidly) I have a clinic, but I'm not getting any clients for my clinic. No clients are coming. If I try to hold classes…*

Gary: Please stop for a minute! I cannot help you create something if you don't stop and take a breath so I can answer the first question you just asked.

Class Participant: *Oh, I'm sorry.*

Gary: You've got to break a little bit. I know in India and Italy and a few other places, people keep on talking until they've said everything they have to say, and everybody else has to figure out what they said, but I don't do it that way. So, first thing. What are you asking for at your clinic every day? Are you asking, "What do I have to be or do to create more people coming in the door than I can handle?" or are you going to "What's wrong? Nobody's coming in the door!"

Class Participant: *The second one.*

Gary: That's a projection and an expectation. You project and expect that nobody's coming in the door and you put that out in the world and the universe says, "Oh, you don't need any more clients."

If I need more clients, I wake up in the morning and say, "Okay, uni-verse, send me some more clients this week." You have to be willing to live from a different point of view.

Class Participant: *Okay.*

Gary: Now go on with the rest of your story.

Class Participant: I'm having the same issue with classes. Nobody is coming for my classes.

Gary: How are you advertising your classes?

Class Participant: Facebook.

Gary: Facebook is not advertising. That's information. Do you have any clients who've done classes with you?

Class Participant: No.

Gary: Do you have anybody who likes you in your clinic?

Class Participant: Yes.

Gary: Okay, call all those people and say, "I'm doing something new. Do you know anybody who might be interested?" Don't ask them if *they're* interested. Ask them if they *know somebody* who might be interested.

Class Participant: Okay.

Gary: When you ask, "Who do you know who might be interested?" they might decide they're interested. But you're not asking them to come to a class. You're asking if they know somebody who might be interested.

And you have to learn to be *interested*. Stop trying to be *interesting*. Most people try to tell you about everything they're doing. I don't do that. I ask them, "What are you doing? What's going on in your life?" Why do I ask that?

Class Participant: So you can deliver a class to them if they ask?

Get People Interested in You by You Being Interested in Them

Gary: No. So they have to reach and ask me a question to see what they can get from me. You're not letting people reach for you. You're trying to reach for them. Which way does the energy go when you're reaching for them? Toward them or away from them?

Class Participant: Toward them.

Gary: If you push energy toward somebody are they going to go toward you or go away?

Class Participant: They're going to go away.

Gary: Yes. You have to pull energy from people. Get them interested in you by being interested in them. I was talking to a man today who just got a job as a substitute teacher. When he goes into a classroom, he tries to learn the names of all the kids so he can call them by their name when he asks them to do something. The kids come up to him and say, "We really like you. You always seem to know our names. It's cool. Nobody else ever bothers."

This guy is not projecting that he's just a substitute teacher. He's projecting that this is a job he wants to do well at. He's not willing for the kids to suffer or for him to suffer. He sits down with them and he says, "Okay, guys. This is the work we have to get done. After we get this done, we'll go outside and play." So the kids sit down and get the work done. No other substitute teacher does that, because none of them are interested in the kids getting their work done, and they're not interested enough to find out what the kids are interested in. What are the kids interested in? Going outside and playing—not sitting in the classroom. This is a place where the substitute teacher is interested in them, and in response to that, the kids are interested in giving to him.

If you're not getting the business you want, if you're not getting everything you desire in life, you're not being *interested.* You're trying to be *interesting,* and you're trying to invite people by showing them all the stuff you know, not by finding out what *they* know, what *they* do, and what's of interest to *them.* You can have that clinic turned around in less than two weeks if you start asking, "What can I be or do today that can create more customers coming in to my shop right away?"

Class Participant: Thank you.

"What Can This Person Actually Hear?"

Class Participant: Sometimes people say things like, "Tell me in thirty seconds what your business is like." I go into a mini-panic about getting it right and summarizing what I do. It's as if they've said, "Tell me the meaning of life in thirty seconds or less." I feel paralysis by analysis just trying to explain it! What would make a difference here?

Gary: What would make a difference is asking: "What can this person hear?" You're trying to explain everything, but they don't want an explanation. They don't really care what you say. That's the reason you've got to ask: "What can this person hear?"

Class Participant: I feel like I'm staring at a blank wall going, "Um..."

Gary: Their head is a blank wall for you because you're not willing to ask, "What can this person hear?" You want to believe that people are interested. There is no possibility they're really interested—because they're saying, "Tell me what you can about your business in thirty seconds." What they really mean is "Get lost, asshole!"

Class Participant: (Laughs) Oh! Right!

Gary: They're not interested in possibilities or anything else. You can say, "Well, I'd love to tell you about my business, but I couldn't do it in thirty seconds, so why don't you tell me what you do?" and watch how quickly they have an answer. They do not wish to listen. They wish to talk!

Class Participant: Thank you for that.

Gary: Do you think people are actually interested? That's a big mistake.

Class Participant: It's about being aware of who wants to know what.

Gary: They have to ask you a real question. "Tell me about your business in thirty seconds" is not a question. It's a demand and a command. Do you like to be commanded?

Class Participant: No, I hate it!

Gary: Then why are you trying to answer that question? You've projected and expected that these people have some interest. They have none!

> Everything that brought up, will you destroy and uncreate it? Right and Wrong, Good and Bad, POD and POC, All 9, Shorts, Boys, and Beyonds.

Class Participant: Gary, could you talk some more about demands and commands? That brought up something, and I haven't quite got a handle on what it is. It definitely pushed a button.

Gary: Yeah, because you're not willing to see when people are giving you a command. You want to believe people are interested in you. Do you want to see how interested people are in you? Walk up to them and say, "Hi. My name's ___. What's yours? What do you do?" and notice how long it takes them to ask you a question about you or your life.

Class Participant: It usually takes a while, if at all. Good point.

Gary: All right, folks, this has been an interesting conversation. Please run:

> What energy, space, and consciousness can I be to live totally without projections, expectations, separations, judgments, and rejections for all eternity? Everything that doesn't allow that to show up, times a godzillion, will you destroy and uncreate it all? Right and Wrong, Good and Bad, POD and POC, All 9, Shorts, Boys, and Beyonds.

Class Participants: Thank you, Gary.

———

All things become possible when you're willing to have the awareness of all things that are possible.

Chapter Five

A CONSTANT STATE OF CREATION

What would it be like if you were willing to create from what you know instead of what everybody else projects and expects you should choose and be?

Gary: Welcome, everyone. Let's start with a question.

All Expectations and Projections Are Limitations

Class Participant: Gary, are all limitations, expectations, and projections just inventions?

Gary: Yes, all projections and expectations are limitations. All limitations are projections and expectations. And all points of view are just an expectation and a projection of what you're supposed to think.

Class Participant: Do we invent those to create what we think?

Gary: You invent them or you buy them, one of the two. I've got a process for you that I came up with in the middle of the night last night.

What have you defined as and of projection and expectation that keeps you continually seeking the need of the limitations of this reality as the maximization of creative capacity that is allowable in this reality? Everything that is times a godzillion, will you destroy and uncreate it all? Right and Wrong, Good and Bad, POD and POC, All 9, Shorts, Boys, and Beyonds.

It's like you're in maximum security mode, folks. You're not willing to have a capacity far beyond this reality, so you need projections and expectations to determine whether you are going beyond this reality.

> What have you defined as and of projection and expectation that keeps you continually seeking the need of the limitations of this reality as the maximization of creative capacity that is allowable in this reality? Everything that is times a godzillion, will you destroy and uncreate it all? Right and Wrong, Good and Bad, POD and POC, All 9, Shorts, Boys, and Beyonds.

When I heard about no projections, expectations, separations, judgments, and rejections, I said, "If those are one of the greatest limitations we have, I'm not going to do that." Every time I found myself doing a projection and expectation I'd say, "POD and POC that." And in so doing, I opened a door to levels of possibility I didn't expect. If you really want to have everything that's possible, you've got to function from this different place.

> What have you defined as and of projection and expectation that keeps you continually seeking the need of the limitations of this reality as the maximization of creative capacity that is permitted in this reality? Everything that is times a godzillion, will you destroy and uncreate it all? Right and Wrong, Good and Bad, POD and POC, All 9, Shorts, Boys, and Beyonds.

"What Do I Really Want to Choose Here?"

You've got to get to the point where you ask: "What do I really want to choose here? What do I really want to create?" You use projections and expectations instead of your capacity to create.

Class Participant: Yesterday I had a meltdown because I realized how much awareness I had cut myself off from because of expectations and projections and how little choice I had on instituting what I desired to create. Now it's like my life is getting recreated based on what I really desire.

Gary: I'm grateful that you're willing to discover what you really desire rather than what you have to come to conclusion about what you desire.

Class Participant: A friend asked me a bunch of questions last night and I realized there are so many things I enjoy doing that I have stopped doing over time, based on other people's projections and expectations about what I should be doing. It's gotten to the point that I don't desire to be or do almost anything I've created in this lifetime. That's both shocking and enlightening.

Gary:

How many projections and expectations are you using to create you as normal, average, real, and the same as everybody else are you choosing? Everything that is times a godzillion, will you destroy and uncreate it all? Right and Wrong, Good and Bad, POD and POC, All 9, Shorts, Boys, and Beyonds.

You have projections and expectations about what you're supposed to look like, feel like, talk like, move like, and think like. How's that working for you?

Class Participant: Not well at all.

Gary: No, it doesn't work.

How many projections and expectations are you using to create you as normal, average, real, and the same as everybody else are you choosing? Everything that is times a godzillion, will you destroy and uncreate it all? Right and Wrong, Good and Bad, POD and POC, All 9, Shorts, Boys, and Beyonds.

How much do you have to expect and project of you that keeps you in a constant state of judgment of you so you can pretend that you might someday turn out like everybody else? Could you really do that? No!

Expectations about Aging

I recently bought a 1990 Mercedes convertible, which I am now selling. It's more than twenty-six years old, it's still beautiful, and it's only got 31,000 miles on it. Recently I was driving the car with Simone. I went around a corner, stomped on it, and squealed down the road. Simone said, "I love the way you drive!"

I said, "Yeah, I'm an old man who still drives well, because I don't project and expect what I'm supposed to be at a certain age."

My dresser came to see me today and she said, "You're my oldest client."

I said, "What?"

She said, "You're my oldest client, but you dress really well."

I said, "Okay, thanks." Interesting. I'm her oldest client. The worst part about it is that she doesn't know how old I actually am. I told her, "I am seventy-plus, but I'm never telling you how many pluses, so don't ask me."

We age our bodies and our minds with projections and expectations about how we're supposed to be and what's supposed to occur when we get to a certain age. We create wrinkles in our faces, sags in our butts, and drags in our bellies. These are all the things we don't like about our bodies getting older, and they're all projections and expectations of what's supposed to happen when you get to the age you happen to be.

> All of the projections and expectations destroying your body, will you destroy and uncreate them all? Right and Wrong, Good and Bad, POD and POC, All 9, Holy Moly! Shorts, Boys, and Beyonds.

Communion with the Earth

Class Participant: You have talked about how we have to have communion with our body and the Earth. Can you say some more about that?

Gary: If you're doing projections and expectations, you cannot have total communion with the Earth, which is one of the reasons we're doing this call.

> How many projections and expectations do you have that you are using to kill the Earth? Everything that is times a godzillion, will you destroy and uncreate it all? Right and Wrong, Good and Bad, POD and POC, All 9, Shorts, Boys, and Beyonds.

Did you sense the energy that came up when I asked that question?

Class Participant: Oh, yeah.

Gary: That means you're aware that you have projections and expectations, but nobody ever asked you, "Are you killing the Earth with those?"

Class Participant: I had no idea.

Gary: If you become aware of this, you'll have more possibilities. Things will show up that will create more for you and the rest of mankind.

How many projections and expectations do you have that are killing the Earth? Everything that is times a godzillion, will you destroy and uncreate it all? Right and Wrong, Good and Bad, POD and POC, All 9, Shorts, Boys, and Beyonds.

We're tapping into a lot of past lives here. Many of you have used projections and expectations to create your share of the market and your share of the money on planet Earth. If you didn't do that, what other choices might you have?

Everything that is times a godzillion, will you destroy and uncreate it all? Right and Wrong, Good and Bad, POD and POC, All 9, Shorts, Boys, and Beyonds.

The Intensity of Space

Class Participant: In the Access Level 2 and 3 Manual[4]*, it says that you can either live from projections, expectations, separations, judgments, and rejections or from the intensity of space that doesn't allow limitation to exist. Can you talk about the intensity of space?*

Gary: Intensity of space is what occurs when you no longer have any need, desire, want, or require of any kind of projection or expectation. Let me ask you something: If you're with a woman who projects and expects that you should be choosing her to have a relationship with, do you have any space?

Class Participant: No.

---

[4] The *Access Level 2 and 3 Manual* has been changed to *Choice of Possibilities*.

Gary: Are you spending your time asking, "What can I create with this person?" or are you spending your time asking, "How do I get away from her?"

Class Participant: The second one, probably.

Gary: And when you find somebody who's actually fun to play with, you have a different energy.

Class Participant: Yes.

Gary: That's your energy being you. That's the intensity of space that is actually possible for you. And you do that, even though you don't think you know how to do it.

Class Participant: Cool. Then you ask: "What can I create now?"

Gary: That's where choice comes in.

The Projection and Expectation of a Reality That Doesn't Actually Exist

Class Participant: This morning I realized I have expectations of Access, I have expectations of my life, I have expectations of my body, and I have expectations of my classes. It was "Oh my God! I've been living a life of expectations!" Expectation extends to every area of my life. I began to destroy and uncreate them and I got a glimpse of the freedom you have, which is phenomenal. The question is: Where else am I stopping myself? Is there a clearing for everything, including expectations we might have of you, or Access, or a class?

Gary: Projections and expectations create a place where you have to go to separation, judgment, or rejection, primarily of you. If you do projection or expectation of anything, you have to reject and separate or judge the other person or yourself—one of the two. Neither one creates a place where there's a possibility and choice in reality.

What have you made so vital about projection, expectation, separation, judgment, and rejection that keeps you eternally seeking life based on what you cannot choose? Everything that is times a godzillion, will you destroy and uncreate all that? Right and Wrong, Good and Bad, POD and POC, All 9, Shorts, Boys, and Beyonds.

Class Participant: I've been looking at the ideas of fairness, earning, and deserving and how I'm still functioning from those concepts. What is required to let go of those in totality?

Gary: You are projecting and expecting a reality that doesn't actually exist. *Fairness, earning,* and *deserving* are projections and expectations of a world that is based on equality, truth, and awareness. A bird is sitting in a tree and suddenly a cat pounces on it. Is that fairness? Is that earning? Is that deserving? Those concepts of reality aren't actually true or real.

You've got to see the reality *you are in,* not the reality *you would like to be in.*

> What have you made so vital about *fairness, earning,* and *deserving* that keeps you eternally in the projection and expectation of something that cannot exist in this reality? Everything that is times a godzillion, will you destroy and uncreate it all? Right and Wrong, Good and Bad, POD and POC, All 9, Shorts, Boys, and Beyonds.

While we're at it, you need to get that with the way things are set up in this reality, you as an infinite being cannot exist.

> How many projections and expectations do you have of you that keep you from existing in this reality? Everything that is times a godzillion, will you destroy and uncreate it all? Right and Wrong, Good and Bad, POD and POC, All 9, Shorts, Boys, and Beyonds.

Class Participant: You've talked about how you, personally, create beyond this reality and how you also use this reality. How does that work with this clearing?

Gary: Somewhere you have a point of view that you're supposed to function *with* this reality and you're supposed to exist *in* this reality. Is that real? No, it's not real. You keep thinking that if you can somehow function here in this reality then you will exist here. Does that acknowledge you as an infinite being? No. Let's say your parents have a projection and expectation of you. Can you live by that?

Class Participant: Not at all.

Gary: If this reality has a projection and expectation of you, can you live *by* that—or *with* that?

Class Participant: I think you can live with *it but not* by *it.*

Gary: Living with it requires you to invalidate a huge amount of *you.* Don't try to live with it. You have to use it without living with it. You've got to ask: "Am I doing an expectation and projection of something? How can I use this to my advantage?" You've got to be willing to take advantage of people who live from the point of view of what they think *should be* instead of *what is.*

Class Participant: This is a real game changer. Thank you very much.

Gary:

> What projection and expectation of a reality that actually doesn't exist are you using to keep you from being? Everything that is times a godzillion, will you destroy and uncreate it all? Right and Wrong, Good and Bad, POD and POC, All 9, Shorts, Boys, and Beyonds.

As an infinite being, would you have an awareness of what could be?

Class Participant: Yes.

Gary: Are you trying not to have that awareness? You have to look at a reality that *could* exist and ask, "*Does* this exist?" The point of view "only if I choose it" doesn't work. Why don't you want to have that reality? Because nobody else can align and agree with an awareness that is beyond this reality. And if you don't have alignment and agreement with others, you think you are being separate rather than recognizing you're creating a future that currently doesn't exist.

Class Participant: Oh, wow!

Gary: Projections and expectations create the point of view you're supposed to live by. How many projections and expectations are you using to live by that don't actually create living? You don't get that you have to look from a different point of view to create a reality that is not part of this reality's point of view.

> How many projections and expectations are you using that you are trying to live from that actually don't create living? Everything that is times a godzillion, will you destroy and uncreate it all? Right and Wrong, Good and Bad, POD and POC, All 9, Shorts, Boys, and Beyonds.

Are You Expecting Problems?

Class Participant: Recently I set up a website. I keep changing the content because I don't want people to take the point of view that I can't work with their needs. How do you stay in a question when you're setting up a website?

Gary: Where did you come to the point of view that people won't be able to receive what you are offering?

Class Participant: Well, maybe that's an expectation on my side of things.

Gary: Yes, that's a projection and an expectation. I don't project and expect that anybody's going to hear ninety-nine percent of what I say.

Class Participant: (Laughs) Okay. I can align with that.

Gary: You don't have to align with it. Just be aware. One of the things you've learned in this reality is that you must anticipate problems. That's projection and expectation.

Recently somebody told us that another person was openly selling CDs of the Access classes she'd taken to pay for her next classes.

I said, "Really?" I sent a letter to her asking, "How is this honoring of Access? And how is this honesty to you? Why would you do this? If this is what you're going to do, you're going to be hearing from my attorney." After a short period of time, this lady got back to me and said, "I didn't do this."

It turned out that the person complaining about what she was doing didn't have all the information. People tend to go off half-cocked. They project and expect problems before they actually ask, "Is this a problem?" You've got to be willing to recognize the projections and expectations people are operating from. You've got to look at everything that's going on all the time.

If you reference from projections and expectations alone, you're always going to see a problem. One of the things I have to do in business is check with the powers that are in my world and ask: "Is this possible? Is this what's going on? What do we need to be aware of here and what do we need to change?"

How many projections and expectations of problems are you using to create the problems you are choosing? Everything that doesn't allow you to ask that question, will you destroy and uncreate it all? Right and Wrong, Good and Bad, POD and POC, All 9, Shorts, Boys, and Beyonds.

If you had no projection or expectation, you'd look at something and ask: "Is this a problem?" But if you're already projecting and expecting problems, guess what's going to show up in your life? Problems!

A Constant State of Creation

When we were in Costa Rica for facilitators training, everybody was talking about the fact that we had started an online school for kids in first to eighth grade but no one had signed up. People were asking, "What are we going to do?"

I said, "Close it down."

Everyone said, "What?!"

I said, "Close it down."

And then someone said, "My son, who's in high school, wanted to sign up for the school because it would be right up his alley, but it was only offered for younger kids."

I said, "So let's make it for high school kids. We had talked about having Spanish classes, so we turned it into a language school. We'll probably take high school seniors on board and work backwards to the younger guys.

It totally changed because there was no projection and expectation about how it had to be. It became a different school and people signed up. Okay, cool! This is the way things should be for our whole lives. We should constantly be in a state of creation rather than a state of projection and expectation.

How many projections and expectations are you using to avoid the creation you could be choosing? Everything that is times a godzillion, will you destroy and uncreate it all? Right and Wrong, Good and Bad, POD and POC, All 9, Shorts, Boys, and Beyonds.

If you make a decision that something should look a certain way, can you have a different point of view? No. Every decision you make is based on a projection or expectation—or it creates a projection or expectation.

How many projections and expectations are you using to avoid the creation you could be choosing? Everything that is times a godzillion, will you destroy and uncreate it all? Right and Wrong, Good and Bad, POD and POC, All 9, Shorts, Boys, and Beyonds.

When you get rid of your need of projection and expectation, it puts you in a constant state of create.

Class Participant: What would it take to be there—and just create? Choice, right?

Gary: You could ask: "Is that a projection and an expectation or is it a choice?" Probably a better question to ask is: "Is this a result or a possibility?"

Class Participant: Oh. Nice!

Gary: When what you want is a result, run: "Everything that is and everything that creates that and all the projections and expectations, POC and POD. What's possible here I have not yet chosen?"

Class Participant: Thank you, Gary.

Expectations, Targets, and Results

Class Participant: I notice that the word results has a "blurgh" energy around it. Can you talk about expectations versus targets for businesses?

Gary: Results feels like what you thought you had to do in order to get to where somebody else wanted you to be.

All of the projections and expectations you've used in any lifetime to create all the results you've ever created, will you destroy and uncreate all that? Right and Wrong, Good and Bad, POD and POC, All 9, Shorts, Boys, and Beyonds.

Class Participant: What's the difference between a target and a result? Is a target like the fun of shooting for something? And a result is the goal?

Gary: An example of this is what happened with the online school. That was a target. When you don't have the projection and expectation or the need of a result, the ability to change or create something greater is always available. But every time you have a projection or expectation, you eliminate as many possibilities as you possibly can, because the only thing that is going to happen is what you projected or expected. When you get rid of your need of projection and expectation, it puts you in a constant state of create.

Projections and Expectations about Learning

Class Participant: I love the power of possibilities with the language school. My awareness is that everyone should go. I think that kids learn very well when they are young...

Gary: Hold, hold, hold. How many projections and expectations do you have that learning should be done when kids are young?

Everything that is, will you destroy and uncreate it all? Right and Wrong, Good and Bad, POD and POC, All 9, Shorts, Boys, and Beyonds.

Class Participant: What I meant to say was that my first language was French. I started off in the world speaking French. I don't even remember learning how to speak English. It was so automatic. I was a toddler, and English just came. That's how it was for everyone. When my kids were in grammar school, they learned languages early. My awareness around that was that they picked them up so quickly and easily.

Gary: Hold on a minute. You just said it again, "They learned languages early." How many projections and expectations are you using to create that as a reality?

The expectation that you can learn languages more easily when you're young does not acknowledge that you, personally, are so unique that things might be different for you, and a future might be possible for you that nobody else can have.

Class Participant: Wow. Thank you.

Hypervigilance

Class Participant: What is the difference between hypervigilance, being aware, and creating something without expectation and projection?

Gary: Hypervigilance is the projection and expectation that you are not aware. If you're willing to be totally aware, do you need to be hypervigilant?

Class Participant: No.

Gary: As I was talking with some people today, a bird landed outside the window where I have a fountain. The bird was doing its thing out there. I said, "Look at that cute bird." One of the guys I was talking with said, "Oh, that's a wren. You can always tell because they put their tail up and then they sing."

I said, "Oh, I just learned something." I wasn't being hypervigilant. I was talking with those people and being extremely aware. I do not cut off awareness while I am talking. How many of you project and expect that if you don't pay attention, you won't know what somebody said? You've learned to be hypervigilant because you were punished for not being hypervigilant, weren't you?

Class Participant: Yes.

Gary:

> Everything you've done to make that so much greater than it deserves to be, will you destroy and uncreate all that? Right and Wrong, Good and Bad, POD and POC, All 9, Shorts, Boys, and Beyonds.

Choosing Ten Seconds at a Time Is Living in the Moment

Class Participant: I notice that when I'm choosing ten seconds at a time, I am creating. I get a lot done really quickly, but if I have a "deadline" or something I've committed to do by a certain time, I avoid it like the plague and get unhappy about it.

Gary: Hold, hold, hold. What did you say about being committed?

Class Participant: When I'm working with other people and I commit to delivering something in a certain timeframe…

Gary: That's a projection and expectation that you solidify as a reality. It's not a choice any longer.

Class Participant: If you're working with other people and there are certain deliverables, how do you work that out with no expectations or projections or schedules?

Gary: Someone once said to me, "If you don't project and expect, people won't deliver anything."

I said, "People deliver not because you project and expect; people deliver because they want to do something for you and because they care about you. If you project and expect that they need to do it, the commitment you're demanding of them will require them to resist. It's about choice. What do you want to choose here?

Class Participant: Thank you. I'm getting that it's a self-imposed scale that I've created, and it cuts off my creative capacity when I do that.

Gary: That's the thing about commitment. You think commitment means "I have to do this" not "What do I want to create here?"

Class Participant: I agree with you. This is really big in my universe. What's required for me to change this?

Gary: Ask: "What invention am I using to create the commitment I am choosing?" You're inventing that you have to have a commitment. You're inventing that you are committed. You're inventing that commitment is going to create something. Commitment only creates you in a jail or a lunatic asylum!

Class Participant: I'm grateful for this. When I choose ten seconds at a time, I can create miracles and magic and when I don't do that, it gets awful.

Gary: Yes, because choosing ten seconds at a time is living in the moment. Commitment is based on the projection and expectation that you have to get it done. You make a commitment in order to complete what you started. Do you really have to complete what you started? No. None of it has to do with the creative capacity that is natural and true for you.

Class Participant: I realize I've been giving my word to do things but I have not been aware of what I really desire when I give my word.

Gary: I'm always aware of what I desire before I give my word.

Class Participant: This is the thing that's been creating a snafu for me. What's required to change it?

Gary: You have to give up the projections and expectations that other people desire the same thing you do. You keep assuming they desire what you do, so you think that if you commit to something, they will commit as well. It's a projection and expectation that your commitment is going to create their commitment. I never have that point of view. My commitment is to me—not to them.

Class Participant: Wow. Is this just the bad training of this reality?

Gary: It's that, but it's also the place where you don't get the choice you actually have and how it might work for you.

Class Participant: Right. I have not seen that.

Gary: You project and expect that if you commit to something, other people will too. I don't do that—ever! I have no projections and expectations that anybody will ever complete anything! And because of that, I'm always really happy with what they do create.

Class Participant: (Laughs) I love that! Brilliant.

Gary: I don't project and expect that I'm going to do something perfect. I just ask, "What choices do I have here? What would I like to create? What would I like to do? What would make me happy?" You guys never ask what would make you happy. You always project and expect what's going to make somebody else happy and then you try to choose that.

Class Participant: I've been asking questions about what's outside of me rather than asking what is actually true for me. That is what is changing.

Creating Real Change

Gary: I got an email from a guy who told me that when he was a young man he thought he could change anything. An old man said to him, "You think you can change anything? Cool. I like your enthusiasm. Here's a glass of water. Stick your finger in it. Okay, now take your finger out. Is the hole still there?"

No. So do we really change things? Or do we have to change the chemical composition of something if we want to create a real change? Do we have to change the energetics of something in order to create a real change?

We think we're going to make a change by our enthusiasm or our projections and expectations rather than realizing our projections and expectations are the finger that dips in the water. When you take it out, there's no hole. Everything comes back together as it was. How much effect can you have on the world if you're doing projections and expectations? Zero. Nada. None.

> What are you not willing to be that if you would be it would eliminate the projections and expectations of what you have to be that are keeping you from creating your reality? Everything that is times a godzillion, will you destroy and uncreate it all? Right and Wrong, Good and Bad, POD and POC, All 9, Shorts, Boys, and Beyonds.

When you're young, you're very enthusiastic about what you think you can change. For example, many of you had enthusiasm for the online school we talked about. Did that enthusiasm change people's reality and make it come together? No. But once you were willing to change anything, did that create a different reality? Yes!

Be willing to always change everything and different realities will show up for you because you're willing to change. Okay, we're going to end on that note. Live with that wedgie and see how you come out.

Class Participants: Thank you, Gary.

Gary: Bye.

———

When you get rid of your need of projections and expectations, it puts you in a constant state of create.

Chapter Six

CHOOSING TO BE EVERYTHING YOU ARE

What if you were the best thing that ever happened on planet Earth? All the projections and expectations you've defined as meaningful keep you from being everything you are.

Gary: Hello, everyone. I'd like to start by reading a question that has come in.

Humans and Humanoids

Question: When I started doing Access and found out that there are humans and humanoids, I began to have a lot of projections and expectations, separations, judgments, and rejections about humans. I'd go into conclusions about what a human would do or not do, be or not be. Can you talk about this, please, and give me some clearings for this?

Gary: There are two species of two-legged beings on this planet. We call them humans and humanoids. They look alike, they walk alike, they talk alike, and they often eat alike, but the reality is they're different.

Humanoids are always looking at things and asking, "How can we change that? What will make this better? How can we out do this?" They're the people who have created all the great art, all the great literature, and all the great progress on the planet. Humanoids tend to think that they're not enough and what they choose is never enough, so they're always looking for how to create more. They don't know how to be satisfied with limitation.

Humans will always tell you how *you're* wrong, how *they're* right, and how you shouldn't change anything. They say things like, "We don't do things that way, so don't even bother." Humans are the ones who ask, "Why are you changing that? It's fine the way it is." They say, "You shouldn't worry about this. Everything's all right. It's always been all right. Nothing is a problem." That's the difference between a human and a humanoid.

Going to conclusions about what a human would do or not do, be or not be, is not being aware. You have to look at someone and ask: "Is this person human? Yes. Okay. What will they create? What will they choose? What will they do?" Those questions lead to possibility. If you're not willing to ask those questions, all you'll have are projections and expectations.

How many projections and expectations do you have of humans that keep you in the separations, judgments, and rejections of you that you are choosing? Everything that is times a godzillion, will you destroy and uncreate it all? Right and Wrong, Good and Bad, POD and POC, All 9, Shorts, Boys, and Beyonds.

What Constitutes Reality?

Class Participant: Is it just about POD and POCing any reality, no matter what the reality is?

Gary: What constitutes reality?

Class Participant: Exactly!

Gary: The thing that constitutes reality is two or more people agreeing with your point of view. Don't look for the agreement that allows you to continue to do what isn't working. Why would you want to continue with what isn't working? When you do that, you're creating something as a *result* rather than a *possibility*.

You have to ask: "What question can I be or do or have or create or generate that would take this beyond my awareness? What is possible that I haven't considered?"

Class Participant: Thank you. And would that eliminate the "I'm never enough" loop that we humanoids go into?

Gary: Yes. That would eliminate the loop, "I'm never enough. What's the matter with me?" You're aware of things that you don't even want to know you're aware of, because if you knew you were aware of them, you wouldn't be able to make your life a pile of shit!

"Does Any of This Belong to Me?"

Class Participant: I felt really good after the last two calls. Everything seemed to be new. Today I woke up and I was in judgment and wrongness. I thought, "What the hell is going on here?" I don't understand why I am feeling so bad.

Gary: Can you stop for just one minute? "What the hell is going on here?" is not a question. A question would be "Does any of this belong to me?"[5] If you felt light and good yesterday, none of this stuff you're feeling today belongs to you. You wake up with it every morning, so you assume it must belong to you. If you invite a strange woman into your bed and you wake up with her in the morning, does it mean she belongs to you?

Class Participant: No.

Gary: Does it mean you belong to her?

Class Participant: No. I asked, "Who does this belong to?" and I got the awareness that it isn't mine. I tried to send it back…

Gary: All you have to do is acknowledge that it's not yours. You don't have to do anything with it. It's "Oh! This isn't mine!" When your partner's in bed with you and she farts, do you feel like it's your fart?

---

[5] What if you are way more psychic than you think? What if you are simply assuming that all the thoughts, feelings and emotions you experience are yours? What if they're not? Whose life are you living, anyway? In Access, we have the point of view that the thoughts, feelings, and emotions you experience aren't yours. You can try this out. When you are having a thought, feeling, or emotion, ask: "Who does this belong to?" If it feels lighter when you ask that, the thought, feeling, or emotion is not yours.

Class Participant: No.

(Laughter)

Gary: Okay. Thoughts are like farts. Thoughts are the un-smelly farts of your reality. You don't have to do anything with them. You've got to get this. When you create on a moment-by-moment basis, it's done from the choice and the question. If you use choice and question, you are creating moment by moment. You have to have a question. Projection and expectation are not sources of creation. They are sources of limitation.

> How many projections and expectations are you using to create the limitations you are choosing? Everything that is times a godzillion, will you destroy and uncreate it all? Right and Wrong, Good and Bad, POD and POC, All 9, Shorts, Boys, and Beyonds.

"I Always Feel Judged"

Class Participant: When I'm at home or when I'm facilitating someone, I feel like myself—but if I go outside, if I'm at school or somewhere else, I always feel judged by people.

Gary: You're saying, "When I leave home, I lose me." But you cannot lose you unless you have a projection and expectation that you cannot be you except when you're at home or when you're facilitating someone. You have the projection and expectation, so you have to separate, judge, and reject you based on the awareness you have of how other people function.

Not many people in the world are happy. Not many people in the world actually know who the hell they are. Not many people even want to know who they are. You have the ability to know who you are, but you keep saying there's something wrong with you, which, by the way, is a projection and an expectation.

> How many projections and expectations do you have to create the wrongness of you? Everything that is times a godzillion, will you destroy and uncreate it all? Right and Wrong, Good and Bad, POD and POC, All 9, Shorts, Boys, and Beyonds.

Class Participant: Thank you.

The Limitations You've Created Your Life From Are Brilliant

Class Participant: I'm getting quite clear that any time I'm in judgment of me, it's not going to work. I would judge me for what reason?

Gary: Judgment does not create. It destroys.

Class Participant: And it's a kink in the flow of energy. So projection, expectation, conclusion, rejection, and separation are a judgment used to stop me from being?

Gary: Yep. Isn't that great? It is great because that means you have tremendous power. You've got to see the greatness in that power—or you will create the wrongness of it!

Class Participant: Oh. Then everything we do is great?

Gary: That is correct. Everything you do is great. Everything you choose is great. The question is "Is this all I wish to create? Or do I wish to create more?"

Class Participant: You're so brilliant.

Gary: I am. And I'm willing to acknowledge it.

Class Participant: I'm getting to see how brilliant I am every day.

Gary: You've got to recognize that the limitations you've created your life from are brilliant! Nobody else could make you that screwed up when you're not.

Class Participant: If I'm that powerful, what else is possible?

Gary: Yeah. What else is possible? If I'm this great and this powerful, what would happen if I used it to create and generate a different possibility?

Class Participant: And the only chance for a different possibility is not to stop me, because I don't even know where I can go or how fast I can be.

Gary: Yes. Your life is about "What do I want to create? What do I truly want to create?" You are looking at the choices you make as wrong. What if they were never wrong and they were never right?

The Difference Between Creation and Destruction Is Your Point of View

Class Participant: I just said that judgment is a kink in the flow of energy as a negative. I love how you changed it from a negative to a different point of view.

Gary: That's an ability you need to have.

Class Participant: One is destruction. One is creation.

Gary: That's all there is to it. The difference between creation and destruction is your point of view. What if you didn't think being kinky was a wrong thing? *Kinky* is the willingness to create beyond the limitations of this reality. You wouldn't desire to be kinky for what reason? But you have all these projections and expectations about the separations, judgments, and rejections that will occur if you become what you are.

Everything that is times a godzillion, will you destroy and uncreate it all? Right and Wrong, Good and Bad, POD and POC, All 9, Shorts, Boys, and Beyonds.

What if you were the best thing that ever happened on planet Earth?

Class Participant: Yeah, baby!

Gary: Yeah baby, I'm a kinko. I'm not just a humanoid. I'm a kinkoid.

(Laughter)

"Thank God I Saw This Limitation!"

Class Participant: You've asked us, "What if you were the greatest gift on planet Earth?" Are you saying that when we see a limitation in our world, we need to automatically go to the joy of the awareness that we've seen it? Is that correct?

Gary: Yeah. "Thank God, I saw this limitation! Now what would I like to choose?"

Class Participant: In the past when I've gone to a class and found a limitation, I've said, "Shit! I've got to overcome this or fix it!" Is that the limitation rather than the joy of awareness?

Gary: That's an expectation that the limitation is stronger and greater than you are.

Class Participant: So you view a limitation as great simply because you've seen it?

Gary: Because you've spotted it. "Wow, this is a limitation. Never mind, next choice."

Class Participant: And it's just a choice to start doing that from the joy of awareness?

Creating Beyond Limitation

Gary: Yes, the only innate capacity we have is the ability to choose. You can choose to judge you and make sure everything is a judge-able offense. Or you can choose to create beyond limitation by being willing to perceive, know, be, and receive the limitation.

I have a large sculpture I bought in Bali. It's a bunch of monkeys, with their tails going in all different directions, in twirls and swirls. It was once a giant tree that was destroyed to create something beautiful. When I bought it, it was unbelievably filthy. It was dusty and hideous, so I took it outside and sprayed it off with water and all the curlicues on it turned out to be green with gold tips on them. The eyes of the monkeys came to light, their tails showed up, and their hands became visible. It turned out to be an amazing jumble of monkeys among the trees. Now it is a beautiful thing. People say, "That's so beautiful!" and I say, "Thank you."

When you see the world, be willing to look at it and ask, "What can I change here?" In the act of changing it, it becomes a thing of beauty. I was willing to see the sculpture as the gift it is from the energy somebody used to create it. Someone spent a year, maybe two, carving this thing. Every time I look at it, I see something I haven't seen before. Is that because I'm not willing to be aware, because all of that was always there? Or is it because when you admire something, it becomes greater?

Class Participant: Wow.

Are You Going to Create or Obviate?

Class Participant: I've noticed that if I cook a meal just to get some food on the table, I don't enjoy it. But when I take pleasure in the process of cooking, I have fun through the whole meal and other people enjoy it too.

Gary: It's a shift in your point of view to gratitude. You're grateful for the gift you've been given to create. Most people cook because they have to, not because it's a great joy to share with somebody the gift called them. When people are willing to share the gift called them in the cooking they do, they create a different possibility and a different reality. What would it be like if you were willing to be that gift, that person, and that possibility in everything you do?

> Everything you're unwilling to be, know, perceive, and receive about the choice to create instead of the choice to obviate, will you destroy and uncreate it all? Right and Wrong, Good and Bad, POD and POC, All 9, Shorts, Boys, and Beyonds.

What's the difference between the choice to create and the choice to obviate? The choice to obviate is, "Obviously I have to do this. I have to cook for my family." That's not creating for your family, that's obviating for your family. When you create, you make something that is so amazing that nobody can resist the joy and the energy of the creation.

> Everything you've done to obviate your reality instead of create your reality, will you destroy and uncreate all that? Right and Wrong, Good and Bad, POD and POC, All 9, Shorts, Boys, and Beyonds.

Obviation is when you have to have a result: "If I do this, then this will occur." Creation is "I'm going to choose this and see what shows up." What if you were an excuse to have something different and better?

Class Participant: Can you speak some more to that, please? For example, when you choose to do things because you're looking to change something in your life, is that the choice to create or the choice to obviate? In this reality we operate from wanting to change a specific thing, like a health issue, so we'll go to a health class.

Gary: Are they projections and expectations of what you're going to get? Or is it awareness?

Class Participant: Hmm. Could it be both?

Gary: No. It's always projections and expectations. You go to a class expecting a result. That's a projection and expectation. What if it wasn't about what you expected or what you were going to get?

It's always an expectation and a projection when you do something to get something. "If I do this, I will get that." It's like the way men and women go into marriage. Men go into marriage expecting they are going to get sex. Women do sex expecting they're going to get marriage. How does that work for everybody? It doesn't—because it doesn't have anything to do with creation. You've got to ask: "Am I going to create or obviate?"

> What choice do you have? Creation or obviation? Everything that doesn't allow you to be, know, perceive, and receive that, will you destroy and uncreate it all? Right and Wrong, Good and Bad, POD and POC, All 9, Shorts, Boys, and Beyonds.

Class Participant: When you're using projection and expectation and you don't get the result you were expecting, it's disappointing and demoralizing, but you've created that because you had projections and expectations.

Gary: Isn't that cool? You can create your own disappointment. You've got to ask: "Am I obviating or am I creating?"

Projections and Expectations As the Source of Creation of Relationship

Class Participant: Can you expand on how we reject other people's points of view and what that does energetically for us?

Gary: You try to project and expect that people have some kind of interest in something that you have an interest in, especially if that person is a good-looking guy. I'm not making that wrong. I'm just telling you it's not working. You have an interest in someone, so you're projecting and expecting that they're as interested in you as you are in them. How's that going to work?

> Everything you've done to make your projections and expectations the source of creation of relationship, will you destroy and uncreate

all that? Right and Wrong, Good and Bad, POD and POC, All 9, Shorts, Boys, and Beyonds.

There's a whole different world out there if you're willing to be that different world. If you're not doing the world based on your projections and expectations, you get to see what is in front of you and you get to change anything. But you stop yourself from having it all with your projections and expectations.

Class Participant: It limits me.

Gary: Yes, what would it be like if you were willing to have everything in your life turn out the way you like it?

Class Participant: Is it the willingness to give up the analysis of it and just choose to change it?

Gary: Yes. Ask: "What do I want to choose? How do I want to create this? What would it take to do this?"

Class Participant: Thank you.

Sharing Projections and Expectations

Gary: Here's a question that came in: People always confuse me with what they themselves are doing. And I know it starts with my projections and expectations about them.

Gary: Well, not necessarily. You guys love to share your projections and expectations. How many projections and expectations do you have that you're sharing back and forth, forever, amen? It's like having a pair of dirty underwear that you keep giving to your friend to wear. You don't want to wear them anymore because they're too dirty. So your friend puts them on and says, "Oh no. I don't like these. Here, take them back."

Question: Can you please tell me how to change this? How do I deal with them so I can have ease?

Gary: Say: "Every projection, expectation, separation, judgement, or rejection, I have of this person, I now destroy and uncreate them all." Do this every day, all day long for every person you meet for six months, and you'll be over it.

Needing a Man or a Woman in Your Life

Class Participant: I've been single for two years now. I've tried to change that, but if I'm out with a woman on a date, and she doesn't want anything from me, I feel lighter.

Gary: Is it a projection and expectation that you need a woman in your life?

Class Participant: Yes.

Gary: If you make it about having a woman, then your projection and expectation is that you do not exist without a woman.

How many of you have projections and expectations that you don't exist without a woman in your life or a man in your life? Everything that is times a godzillion, will you destroy and uncreate it all? Right and Wrong, Good and Bad, POD and POC, All 9, Shorts, Boys, and Beyonds.

Class Participant: Ouch.

Gary: Yeah, "Ouch" is right! You're doing all these expectations in life about you've got to have a man or you've got to have a woman, but whatever it is, it's not about how you are so cool. It's about how you're a half being!

All the projections and expectations about how you are a half being if you don't have a woman in your life, will you destroy and uncreate all that? Right and Wrong, Good and Bad, POD and POC, All 9, Shorts, Boys, and Beyonds.

How do people get to be half beings? How can you have a half body, half a being, or half anything? How come you're not a whole anything? You know, the one thing most of you are willing to do is to be right enough to be assholes; a whole ass, at least! And, by the way, you might try being proud of the fact that you can be an asshole.

Be the Asshole You Are and Enjoy It

Class Participant: It's interesting you said that. I'm not opposed to be-ing an asshole. But I think I may have misidentified what being an asshole is. I've spent some time with you and I see that your version of being an asshole is nothing like my version of being an asshole...

Gary: You have serious projections and expectations that lead to sepa-rations, judgments, and rejections of you, from you, in order to prove that you're the asshole you've decided you are, based on other peo-ple's points of view.

You try not to be an asshole instead of enjoying it when you are. You have judgments, separations, and rejections about being an asshole. I don't. For me it's "I'm being an asshole. Like it? No? Too bad."

I'm saying, "Just like it. Just go for it. Or don't like it. Whatever works for you." It's being the asshole you actually are and enjoying it!

For me being an asshole is doing what works for me. I don't do what other people want, the way they want me to do it, at the time they want me to do it. I'm going to be an asshole to get done what I want to get done if that's what's required.

Being an asshole is just a judgment. You guys go into projections and expectations and then the separations, judgments, and rejections about it. I say, "I can be an asshole. What else can I be?"

Class Participant: You use being an asshole to create something greater. That's the difference. Whereas we get stuck in judgment.

Gary: Yes, you use your judgment to reject creation.

Class Participant: Right. And to reject ourselves.

Gary: Yep, isn't it great?

Class Participant: Thank you, Gary.

You Can Only Choose to Be Who and What You Are

Class Participant: You've talked about the time when you got that no one could hear you and that the friends you thought were friends weren't really friends. What kept you going through that time? Was it the awareness of the reality and the future you were creating?

Gary: It was the awareness that I had to have a different reality whether anybody else would or not.

Class Participant: For you.

Gary: For me! I wouldn't do it for anybody else! I was doing it for me.

Class Participant: Well, thank you for doing it for you.

Gary: I'm glad I did, because I can make a whole lot of people more happy, which makes me happy. I never had a projection or expectation that I was going to make anybody happy.

I have a friend who thinks his husband will be happy if he projects and expects himself into what his husband's mother or father is instead of being himself. That doesn't work. People have the projection and expectation that love is what their mother or father do, so their relationships are created from "I'm being like my mother; therefore my husband should love me." Or "I'm being like my father; therefore my husband should love me." That's not the way it works. What creates love for you? What creates love for the other person? That is the question. You cannot make people love you and you cannot make people hate you. You can only choose to be who and what you are.

Being Kind to the Body

Class Participant: What's required to be kind to the body?

Gary: Thanking it for putting up with you is number one! "Body, I'm sorry I was such a jerk to you. What can I change, be, or do that will change all of this for you?"

Class Participant: It almost feels like starting in kindergarten again and recreating how you live your life and how you choose.

Gary: It's called the kindergarten of consciousness.

Class Participant: That's what I feel like right now.

Gary: Well, the good news is, you'll fail at this kindergarten too.

Class Participant: I'm sure I'm supposed to say, "F--k you, Gary!" (Laughs) This whole thing of hoping to be humanoid and making ourselves wrong—what is required to change that?

Gary: Choice. Stop projecting and expecting humans to get you or humanoids to get you. You get you! What if you were willing to be the only person in the world who got you?

Class Participant: Well, I am, for the most part. This is making me laugh, so I will acknowledge that.

Gary: Now we're getting somewhere!

Class Participant: That really eased all the stuff that was welling up. Wow.

Gary: I know, isn't that weird?!

Acknowledging You

Class Participant: Gary, can you do a clearing about acknowledging you and never looking for anyone else to do it?

Gary: It's not about doing a clearing. It's a choice you have to make and an acknowledgment you have to choose. Who's more important to you than you?

Class Participant: Nobody. But I haven't actually acknowledged that.

Gary: You keep looking for somebody else that you can be correct with, or somebody who will love you or get you, or somebody who knows how to do what you know how to do. I don't do that. I figure I'm the only one of my kind. I'm an extinct dinosaur that hatched here on planet Earth and nobody has any idea how I act.

Class Participant: This helps so much, Gary. Thank you.

Gary: I love the fact that you guys keep bringing this stuff up. I'm pleased with these calls. I hope all of you are too, because I want you to eliminate the projections and expectations of what you have to be that are limiting your reality. Projections and expectations are the things you think you have to be, you ought to be, you should be. They're the things that somebody else tells you that you need to be instead of creating your choice or your reality.

Thank you, everyone. Be bad. It's more fun than being good!

―――

You're powerful and you're acting like you're positively pathetic! Don't you get how amazing you actually are?

THE ACCESS CONSCIOUSNESS CLEARING STATEMENT

You are the only one who can unlock the points of view that have you trapped. What I am offering here with the clearing process is a tool you can use to change the energy of the points of view that have you locked into unchanging situations.

Throughout this book, I ask a lot of questions, and some of those questions might twist your head around a little bit. That's my intention. The questions I ask are designed to get your mind out of the picture so you can get to the energy of a situation.

Once the question has twisted your head around and brought up the energy of a situation, I ask if you are willing to destroy and uncreate that energy—because stuck energy is the source of barriers and limitations. Destroying and uncreating that energy will open the door to new possibilities for you.

This is your opportunity to say, "Yes, I'm willing to let go of whatever is holding that limitation in place."

That will be followed by some weird-speak we call the clearing statement:

Right and Wrong, Good and Bad, POD and POC, All 9, Shorts, Boys, and Beyonds.

With the clearing statement, we're going back to the energy of the limitations and barriers that have been created. We're looking at the energies that keep us from moving forward and expanding into all of the spaces that we would like to go. The clearing statement is simply short-speak that addresses the energies that are creating the limitations and contractions in our life.

The more you run the clearing statement, the deeper it goes and the more layers and levels it can unlock for you. If a lot of energy comes up for you in response to a question, you may wish to repeat the process numerous times until the subject being addressed is no longer an issue for you.

You don't have to understand the words of the clearing statement for it to work, because it's about the energy. However, if you're interested in knowing what the words mean, there are some brief definitions given below.

Right and Wrong, Good and Bad is shorthand for: What's right, good, perfect, and correct about this? What's wrong, mean, vicious, terrible, bad, and awful about this? The short version of these questions is: What's right and wrong, good and bad? It is the things that we consider right, good, perfect, and/or correct that stick us the most. We do not wish to let go of them since we decided that we have them right.

POD stands for the **p**oint of **d**estruction; all the ways you have been destroying yourself in order to keep whatever you're clearing in existence.

POC stands for the **p**oint of **c**reation of the thoughts, feelings, and emotions immediately preceding your decision to lock the energy in place.

Sometimes people say "POD and POC it," which is simply shorthand for the longer statement. When you "POD and POC" something, it is like pulling the bottom card out of a house of cards. The whole thing falls down.

All 9 stands for the nine different ways you have created this item as a limitation in your life. They are the layers of thoughts, feelings, emotions, and points of view that create the limitation as solid and real.

Shorts is the short version of a much longer series of questions that include: What's meaningful about this? What's meaningless about this? What's the punishment for this? What's the reward for this?

Boys stands for energetic structures called nucleated spheres. Basically these have to do with those areas of our lives where we've tried to handle something continuously with no effect. There are at least 13 different kinds of these spheres, which are collectively called "the boys." A nucleated sphere looks like the bubbles created when you blow in one of those kids' bubble pipes that has multiple chambers. It creates a huge mass of bubbles, and when you pop one bubble, the other bubbles fill in the space.

Have you ever tried to peel away the layers of an onion when you were trying to get to the core of an issue, but you could never get there? That's because it wasn't an onion; it was a nucleated sphere.

Beyonds are feelings or sensations that stop your heart, stop your breath, or stop your willingness to look at possibilities. Beyonds are what occur when you are in shock. We have lots of areas in our lives where we freeze up. Any time you freeze up, it's a beyond holding you captive. That's the difficulty with a beyond: it stops you from being present. The beyonds include everything that is beyond belief, reality, imagination, conception, perception, rationalization, forgiveness, as well as all the other beyonds. They are usually feelings and sensations, rarely emotions, and never thoughts.

What Is Access Consciousness?

What if you were willing to nurture and care for you?
What if you would open the doors to being everything
you have decided it is not possible to be?
What would it take for you to realize how crucial you are
to the possibilities of the world?

Access Consciousness is a simple set of tools, techniques, and philosophies that allow you to create dynamic change in every area of your life. Access provides step-by-step building blocks that allow you to become totally aware and to begin functioning as the conscious being you truly are. These tools can be used to change whatever isn't working in your life so that you can have a different life and a different reality.

You can access these tools via a variety of classes, books, teleclasses, and other products, or with an Access Consciousness Certified Facilitator or an Access Consciousness Bars Facilitator.

The goal of Access is to create a world of consciousness and oneness. Consciousness is the ability to be present in your life in every moment without judgment of yourself or anyone else. Consciousness includes everything and judges nothing. It's the ability to receive everything, reject nothing, and create everything you desire in life, greater than you currently have and more than you can ever imagine.

Gary M. Douglas

For more information about Access Consciousness, or to locate an Access Consciousness Facilitator, please visit:

www.accessconsciousness.com

or

www.garymdouglas.com